AFRICAN POLITICAL, ECONOMIC, AND SECURITY ISSUES

THE AFRICAN GROWTH AND OPPORTUNITY ACT

PROVISIONS, IMPACT, AND ISSUES

AFRICAN POLITICAL, ECONOMIC, AND SECURITY ISSUES

Additional books in this series can be found on Nova's website under the Series tab.

Additional E-books in this series can be found on Nova's website under the E-book tab.

AFRICAN POLITICAL, ECONOMIC, AND SECURITY ISSUES

THE AFRICAN GROWTH AND OPPORTUNITY ACT

PROVISIONS, IMPACT, AND ISSUES

HOWARD SARISOHN
AND
JONATHAN COHEN
EDITORS

NOVINKA

New York

For permission to use material from this book please contact us:
Telephone 631-231-7269; Fax 631-231-8175
Web Site: http://www.novapublishers.com

Additional color graphics may be available in the e-book version of this book.

Library of Congress Cataloging-in-Publication Data

ISBN: 978-1-62948-299-6

Published by Nova Science Publishers, Inc. † New York

CONTENTS

PREFACE

In 2000, Congress passed the African Growth and Opportunity Act (AGOA), a U.S. trade preference program, in order to help spur market-led economic growth and development in sub-Saharan Africa (SSA) and deepen U.S. trade and investment ties with the region. Since its enactment, Congress has amended AGOA five times, making some technical changes and renewing the trade preferences through September 30, 2015. According to the Assistant U.S. Trade Representative, (USTR) for Africa, "AGOA is the cornerstone of America's trade and investment policy with sub-Saharan Africa." Economic conditions in Africa, however, have changed considerably since Congress passed the initial AGOA legislation. Annual real gross domestic product (GDP) growth in SSA was nearly a full percentage point lower than global GDP growth (2.3% vs. 3.2%) in the decade leading up to AGOA's passage (1990-2000). Over the last ten years, however, SSA's growth averaged 5.7%, two points higher than the 3.7% world average. While the region still contains many of the world's poorest countries and faces significant economic challenges, some observers and policymakers argue that changing economic conditions warrant an evolution in U.S. policy toward SSA, focused more strongly on private sector investment and increasing two-way trade. In recent years, SSA's growing economic potential and abundant natural resources have attracted other foreign investors, including state- supported enterprises from countries such as China, which is now the region's largest trading partner. This book seeks to inform the discussion on the potential reauthorization of AGOA through analysis of: (1) the components of the AGOA legislation; (2) U.S. import trends associated with AGOA; (3) the impact of AGOA on African economies and U.S.-Africa trade; and (4) the issues surrounding the reauthorization process.

Chapter 1 – The African Growth and Opportunity Act (AGOA) is a non-reciprocal trade preference program that provides duty-free treatment to U.S. imports of certain products from eligible sub-Saharan African (SSA) countries. Congress first authorized AGOA in 2000 to encourage export-led growth and economic development in SSA and improve U.S. economic relations with the region. Its current authorization expires on September 30, 2015.

In terms of tariff benefits and general eligibility criteria, AGOA is similar to the Generalized System of Preferences (GSP), a U.S. trade preference program that applies to more than 120 developing countries. AGOA, however, covers more products and includes additional eligibility criteria beyond those in GSP. Additionally, AGOA includes trade and development provisions beyond its duty-free preferences.

U.S. imports from AGOA beneficiary countries (AGOA countries) represent a very small share (2%) of total U.S. imports and are largely concentrated in energy-related products. Oil is consistently the top duty-free U.S. import from AGOA countries, accounting for 86% of such imports in 2012. Among non-energy products, apparel is the top export for a number of AGOA countries. U.S. apparel imports typically face relatively high tariffs and are excluded from duty-free treatment in GSP, but are included in the AGOA preferences giving AGOA countries a competitive advantage over other apparel producers. Still, only a handful of countries, primarily Lesotho, Kenya, and Mauritius, make significant use of the apparel benefits. Apart from apparel and energy products, South Africa accounts for the bulk of U.S. imports under AGOA. As the most economically-advanced country in the region, South Africa also exports a much more diverse range of manufactured goods than other AGOA countries; vehicles in particular have become a major South African export under AGOA.

Most observers agree that AGOA has successfully led to increased and more diversified exports to the United States from sub-Saharan African countries. Despite this, Congress may wish to address a number of issues and challenges as it considers possible reauthorization of AGOA. Among these challenges is how current and potential AGOA beneficiaries can better utilize the AGOA program and its duty-free benefits. Studies suggest that even among some countries that do make significant use of the AGOA preferences, the low-skill apparel production which AGOA has spurred has not led to the production of higher-skill manufactured products. Other issues relate to the non-reciprocal nature of the AGOA preferences. Some argue that the United States should focus more on two-way trade agreements with the region, particularly with more advanced countries such as South Africa, given improving economic conditions in Africa in recent years. The European Union (EU), for example, has negotiated Economic Partnership Agreements (EPAs) with several African countries that provide some reciprocal tariff benefits, potentially placing U.S. firms at a competitive disadvantage relative to European firms in some markets.

Chapter 2 – Following the end of the apartheid era in South Africa in the early 1990s, the United States sought to increase economic relations with sub-Saharan Africa (SSA). President Clinton instituted several measures that dealt with investment, debt relief, and trade. Congress passed legislation that required the President to develop a trade and development policy for Africa.

Between 1960 and 1973, Africa's economic growth was relatively strong, followed by a period of stagnation and decline for the subsequent two decades in many SSA countries. Current perspectives, however, indicate that many of the fastest-growing countries in the world are on the African continent, and the International Monetary Fund (IMF) projects that the SSA region will grow in terms of real GDP by 5.3% in 2012 and 2013.

In 2000, Congress approved new U.S. trade and investment legislation for SSA in the African Growth and Opportunity Act (AGOA; Title I, P.L. 106-200). According to U.S. trade statistics, U.S. trade with SSA has comprised 1% to 2% of U.S. total trade with the world. AGOA extends preferential treatment to U.S. imports from eligible countries that are pursuing market reform measures. Data show that U.S. imports under AGOA are mostly energy products, but imports of other products have grown significantly. AGOA mandated that U.S. officials meet regularly with their counterparts in SSA, and 11 of these meetings have been held to date. The 11th AGOA Forum was held from June 14 to June 15, 2012, in Washington, DC.

AGOA also directed the President to provide U.S. government technical assistance and trade capacity support to AGOA beneficiary countries. Government agencies that have roles in this effort include the U.S. Agency for International Development, the Assistant U.S. Trade Representative for Africa (established by statute under AGOA), the Overseas Private Investment Corporation, the Export-Import Bank, the U.S. and Foreign Commercial Service, and the Trade and Development Agency. In AGOA, Congress declared that free-trade agreements should be negotiated, where feasible, with interested SSA countries. Related to this provision, negotiations on a free-trade agreement with the Southern African Customs Union (SACU), which includes South Africa and four other countries, began in June 2003, but were suspended in April 2006.

The 112th Congress enacted legislation to extend through September 2015 an expiring provision in AGOA, which allows apparel made in lesser-developed countries to be made of yarns and fabrics from any country and still receive duty-free treatment, subject to a cap (P.L. 112-163). This amendment to AGOA also added South Sudan to the list of SSA countries eligible for AGOA benefits. Eligible countries may become AGOA beneficiaries subject to approval by the Administration.

Legislation is pending to further enhance U.S.-SSA trade relations. H.R. 4221 and S. 2215 seek to increase U.S. exports to Africa, in part, through strategies aimed at further developing relationships between the United States and African countries on a government-to-government level, fostering private sector U.S.-African ties, and targeting more U.S. export financing toward trade with Africa. An amended version of S. 2215 was ordered reported by the Senate Foreign Relations Committee in September 2012. H.R. 656, a separate initiative, would create at the State Department a Special Representative for United States-Africa Trade, Development, and Diaspora Affairs that would also promote U.S. trade and investment ties with SSA.

Chapter 3 – Statement of Ambassador Johnnie Carson, Assistant Secretary for African Affairs, U.S. Department of State.

Chapter 4 – Statement of Earl W. Gast, Assistant Administrator for Africa, U.S. Agency for International Development.

Chapter 5 – Statement of Florizelle Liser, Assistant U.S. Trade Representative for Africa, Office of the U.S. Trade Representative.

In: The African Growth and Opportunity Act ISBN: 978-1-62948-299-6
Editors: H. Sarisohn and J. Cohen

Chapter 1

AFRICAN GROWTH AND OPPORTUNITY ACT (AGOA): BACKGROUND AND REAUTHORIZATION*

Brock R. Williams

SUMMARY

The African Growth and Opportunity Act (AGOA) is a non-reciprocal trade preference program that provides duty-free treatment to U.S. imports of certain products from eligible sub-Saharan African (SSA) countries. Congress first authorized AGOA in 2000 to encourage export-led growth and economic development in SSA and improve U.S. economic relations with the region. Its current authorization expires on September 30, 2015.

In terms of tariff benefits and general eligibility criteria, AGOA is similar to the Generalized System of Preferences (GSP), a U.S. trade preference program that applies to more than 120 developing countries. AGOA, however, covers more products and includes additional eligibility criteria beyond those in GSP. Additionally, AGOA includes trade and development provisions beyond its duty-free preferences.

U.S. imports from AGOA beneficiary countries (AGOA countries) represent a very small share (2%) of total U.S. imports and are largely

---

* This is an edited, reformatted and augmented version of a Congressional Research Service publication, CRS Report for Congress R43173, prepared for Members and Committees of Congress, from www.crs.gov, dated August 2, 2013.

concentrated in energy-related products. Oil is consistently the top duty-free U.S. import from AGOA countries, accounting for 86% of such imports in 2012. Among non-energy products, apparel is the top export for a number of AGOA countries. U.S. apparel imports typically face relatively high tariffs and are excluded from duty-free treatment in GSP, but are included in the AGOA preferences giving AGOA countries a competitive advantage over other apparel producers. Still, only a handful of countries, primarily Lesotho, Kenya, and Mauritius, make significant use of the apparel benefits. Apart from apparel and energy products, South Africa accounts for the bulk of U.S. imports under AGOA. As the most economically-advanced country in the region, South Africa also exports a much more diverse range of manufactured goods than other AGOA countries; vehicles in particular have become a major South African export under AGOA.

Most observers agree that AGOA has successfully led to increased and more diversified exports to the United States from sub-Saharan African countries. Despite this, Congress may wish to address a number of issues and challenges as it considers possible reauthorization of AGOA. Among these challenges is how current and potential AGOA beneficiaries can better utilize the AGOA program and its duty-free benefits. Studies suggest that even among some countries that do make significant use of the AGOA preferences, the low-skill apparel production which AGOA has spurred has not led to the production of higher-skill manufactured products. Other issues relate to the non-reciprocal nature of the AGOA preferences. Some argue that the United States should focus more on two-way trade agreements with the region, particularly with more advanced countries such as South Africa, given improving economic conditions in Africa in recent years. The European Union (EU), for example, has negotiated Economic Partnership Agreements (EPAs) with several African countries that provide some reciprocal tariff benefits, potentially placing U.S. firms at a competitive disadvantage relative to European firms in some markets.

INTRODUCTION

In 2000, Congress passed the African Growth and Opportunity Act (AGOA), a U.S. trade preference program, in order to help spur market-led economic growth and development in sub-Saharan Africa (SSA) and deepen U.S. trade and investment ties with the region.[1] Since its enactment, Congress has amended AGOA five times, making some technical changes and renewing the trade preferences through September 30, 2015.

According to the Assistant U.S. Trade Representative, (USTR) for Africa, "AGOA is the cornerstone of America's trade and investment policy with sub-Saharan Africa."[2] Economic conditions in Africa, however, have changed considerably since Congress passed the initial AGOA legislation. Annual real gross domestic product (GDP) growth in SSA was nearly a full percentage point lower than global GDP growth (2.3% vs. 3.2%) in the decade leading up to AGOA's passage (1990-2000).[3] Over the last ten years, however, SSA's growth averaged 5.7 %, two points higher than the 3.7% world average. While the region still contains many of the world's poorest countries and faces significant economic challenges, some observers and policymakers argue that changing economic conditions warrant an evolution in U.S. policy toward SSA, focused more strongly on private sector investment and increasing two-way trade.[4] In recent years, SSA's growing economic potential and abundant natural resources have attracted other foreign investors, including state-supported enterprises from countries such as China, which is now the region's largest trading partner. Some Members of Congress, the Obama Administration, and many African governments have highlighted the successes of AGOA and have called for an expedited reauthorization process. As part of this process, Congress may wish to consider whether AGOA, in its current form, is achieving the initial goals of the program, including whether it addresses effectively the changing economic circumstances in Africa. Most interested observers are positive about the AGOA preference program, but some ha expressed concerns about specific provisions of the program, such as the lack of coverage for certain agricultural products, or would like to see the AGOA preferences granted to a broader range of least-developed countries beyond just Africa. Others would like to see a broader program that addresses concerns over U.S. businesses' ability to effectively compete in the region, though this could also be addressed in complementary legislation or Administrative initiatives.[5] This report seeks to inform the discussion on the potential reauthorization of AGOA through analysis of: (1) the components of the AGOA legislation; (2) U.S. import trends associated with AGOA; (3) the impact of AGOA on African economies and U.S.-Africa trade; and (4) the issues surrounding the reauthorization process.

KEY PROVISIONS OF AGOA[6]

AGOA (Title I, P.L. 106-200), as amended, is a non-reciprocal preference program that provides duty-free access into the United States for qualifying exports from eligible SSA countries. Among the products that qualify for this duty-free treatment, apparel products have particular economic significance for several countries, in part due to special provisions granted to least-developed AGOA countries ("Third-Country Fabric Provision").[7] In addition to the tariff preferences, the AGOA legislation includes mandates for an annual meeting of U.S. and African government officials to discuss trade and economic issues—the AGOA Forum—as well as specific guidelines on U.S. development assistance directed toward SSA. Countries must meet specific eligibility requirements to qualify for these benefits.

Table A-1 in the Appendix, provides a list of SSA countries, as defined by AGOA. It highlights the 39 that are current AGOA beneficiaries, and notes their eligibility status for other aspects of the AGOA preferences and GSP. It also lists U.S. imports under AGOA and GSP for each country and its GDP/capita—a rough measure of a country's level of economic development.

Unilateral Trade Preference Program

At the core of AGOA are the tariff benefits that provide duty-free access to the U.S. market for certain products from eligible SSA countries. In terms of these tariff benefits and country eligibility requirements, AGOA is essentially an expansion of the Generalized System of Preferences (GSP), a U.S trade preference program that applies to over 120 developing countries, including SSA countries. AGOA builds on GSP by providing preferential access to the U.S. market for more products, such as apparel, and sets out additional eligibility criteria. AGOA also includes other trade and development components, beyond preferences, that are not part of GSP.[8]

AGOA, like other U.S. trade preference programs, is non-reciprocal and unilateral. The preferences apply to U.S. imports and not to U.S. exports, so reauthorization only requires action by the U.S. government. These one-way preferences are granted to developing countries with the goal of enhancing export-led economic growth, and typically exclude items that may be considered import sensitive. This distinguishes them from other U.S. trade liberalization efforts such as free trade agreements (FTAs) or multilateral agreements through the World Trade Organization (WTO), which reduce and/or eliminate tariffs for both U.S. imports and exports. AGOA included a provision requiring the President to explore potential FTA negotiations with interested AGOA beneficiaries, suggesting that Congress envisioned AGOA as a stepping stone to potential broader trade pacts with African countries.

FTA negotiations with South Africa and its regional partners in the South African Customs Union (SACU) sprang from this mandate in AGOA, but were ultimately unsuccessful and suspended in 2006.[9]

Product Coverage

The tariff benefits provided by AGOA include all products covered by GSP, as well as additional products the President determines are not import-sensitive with regard to imports from SSA.[10] According to a report by the Government Accountability Office (GAO) in 2008, the U.S. Harmonized Tariff Schedule (HTS) includes some 10,500 individual tariff lines for U.S. goods imports, of which roughly 3,800 have no most-favored nation (MFN) tariff (*i.e.,* all WTO members may export them to the U.S. duty-free).[11] GSP removes the tariff on an additional 3,400 products (4,800 for least-developed countries), and AGOA makes another 1,800 tariff lines duty-free, though a large share of these are included in the GSP benefits for least-developed countries (LDCs).[12]

AGOA extends duty-free treatment to certain apparel and footwear products, which are not eligible under GSP (even for LDCs). Agricultural products subject to tariff-rate quotas (TRQ) remain ineligible for duty-free treatment under both AGOA and GSP.[13] AGOA beneficiaries are also exempt from certain caps on allowable duty-free imports under the GSP program ("competitive need limitations"). [14]

Rules of Origin

Products from AGOA countries must meet certain rules of origin (ROO) requirements in order to qualify for duty-free treatment (see the textiles and apparel section for sector-specific rules of origin). First, duty-free entry is only allowed if the article is imported directly from the beneficiary country into the United States. Second, at least 35% of the appraised value of the product must be the "growth, product or manufacture" of a beneficiary developing country, as defined by the sum of (1) the cost or value of materials produced in the beneficiary developing country (or any two or more beneficiary countries that are members of the same association or countries and are treated as one country for purposes of the U.S. law) plus (2) the direct costs of processing in the country. Up to 15% of the required 35% of the appraised value may be of U.S. origin, and any amount of production in other beneficiary SSA countries may also contribute to the value-added requirement ("regional cumulation").[15]

Textile and Apparel Provisions

AGOA includes duty-free treatment for certain apparel and textile products, though some are subject to quantitative limitations. These provisions in AGOA are significant, because: (1) apparel production has played a unique role in the development process of some countries; and (2) the duty-free benefits apply to a sector with relatively higher U.S. tariff rates than average overall U.S. tariff rates. Not all AGOA beneficiaries are eligible for the apparel provisions. Duty-free treatment for apparel products under AGOA requires beneficiary countries to adopt an efficient visa ("tracking") system to prevent unlawful transshipment—production shipped through and exported from, but not actually produced in, a given country, often for particular tariff or quota benefits.[16]

Apparel production has been a significant component in some countries' economic development.[17] Unlike textile production, it typically requires low-skilled labor and minimal capital expenditures, allowing lesser-developed countries to become globally competitive. Some research suggests that success in low-skill and export intensive industries such as apparel may help lead to a more diversified manufacturing sector.[18] Nonetheless, the U.S. apparel sector is deemed "import sensitive," and has some specific safeguards. For example, in U.S. free trade agreements (FTAs), apparel tariff lines typically have "yarn forward" general rules of origin (which govern how much of the product must be made in the beneficiary country and longer tariff phase outs), and most preference programs either exclude these articles (GSP) or have caps on duty-free treatment (including AGOA).[19]

The existing general restrictions on U.S. imports of apparel make AGOA's preferential treatment for these product lines especially advantageous. The average U.S. applied tariff on apparel is 11.4% compared to an average for all products of 3.5%.[20] This relatively high preference margin may help explain how some AGOA producers, especially the LDCs, are competitive with lower-cost producers in Asia and elsewhere.[21]

Textile and apparel articles qualifying for duty-free treatment include:

- Apparel assembled in one or more AGOA beneficiary countries from U.S. yarn and fabric;
- Apparel made of SSA (regional) yarns and fabrics, subject to a cap until 2015;
- Apparel made in a designated LDC of third-country yarns and fabrics, subject to a cap until 2015;

- Apparel made of yarns and fabrics not produced in commercial quantities in the United States (determination must be made that the yarn or fabric cannot be supplied by the U.S. industry in a timely manner, and to extend preferential treatment to the eligible fabric);
- Certain cashmere and merino wool sweaters;
- Textiles and textile articles produced entirely in an LDC SSA beneficiary country; and
- Certain handloomed, handmade, ethnic printed fabrics, or folklore articles (certain countries only).[22]

Third-Country Fabric Provision

AGOA's third-country fabric provision is a special rule that allows U.S. apparel imports from least-developed SSA countries to qualify for duty-free treatment even if the yarns and fabrics used in the production of the apparel are imported from non-AGOA countries. This provision, which was reauthorized in August 2012 (P.L. 112-163), is currently set to expire in September 2015, along with the overall AGOA program.

Eligibility

Eligibility for the AGOA trade preference program consists of two separate steps. First, the country must be included in a statutorily-created list of sub-Saharan African countries, described in AGOA (19 U.S.C. 3706). This list has been updated periodically by new legislation (*e.g.*, the 112th Congress added South Sudan in P.L. 112-163).

The second step requires the President to determine annually which eligible countries, from those on the list of SSA countries defined by Congress, should become beneficiaries of the AGOA preferences. There are two different sets of criteria for the President's consideration in this process: Section 104 of AGOA (19 U.S.C. 3703) and Section 502 of the Trade Act of 1974, or GSP (19 U.S.C. 2462).

- *Section 104* is specific to AGOA and requires the President to consider a number of factors related to the prospective AGOA country's economy; rule of law; elimination of barriers to U.S. trade and investment; poverty reduction efforts; protection of worker rights;

support of terrorist activities; and interference with U.S. national security and foreign policy efforts.

- *Section 502*, as amended, sets out the eligibility requirements of the Generalized System of Preferences (GSP), which must also be met by any AGOA beneficiary country. These also include a number of economic and political factors.

At the conclusion of the most recent annual review on December 20, 2012, President Obama issued a proclamation in which, among other things, he revoked AGOA eligibility for Mali and Guinea-Bissau, and granted it to South Sudan.

Least-Developed Country Status

AGOA, like GSP, has additional benefits for least-developed beneficiary countries (LDCs). Under GSP, these countries qualify for duty-free treatment on an additional 1,400 products. Under AGOA, the additional benefits are more flexible rules governing the duty-free treatment of textiles and apparel. Unlike GSP, which provides the President broad latitude in determining LDC status, AGOA defines LDCs as countries with a per capita gross national product (GNP) of less than $1,500 in 1998 as measured by the World Bank.[23] Botswana, Namibia, and Mauritius are also explicitly granted LDC status in AGOA, despite GNP per capita levels above that threshold. This exemption is particularly economically significant for Mauritius; it is the fourth-largest exporter under AGOA (excluding oil trade) and exports primarily apparel products under the preference program.

AGOA Forum

AGOA requires the President, in consultation with Congress and the other governments concerned, to hold annually a United States-Sub-Saharan Africa Trade and Economic Cooperation Forum.[24] The purpose of the Forum, which is held in alternate years in the United States and Africa, is to "discuss expanding trade and investment relations between the United States and Sub-Saharan Africa and the implementation of [AGOA] including encouraging joint ventures between small and large businesses." The 12th AGOA Forum is being held in Addis Ababa, Ethiopia, August 12-13, 2013. The theme for this year's event is "Sustainable Transformation through Trade and Technology."

Technical Assistance and Capacity Building

Unlike other U.S. preference programs, AGOA directs the President to target U.S. government technical assistance and trade capacity building (TCB) in AGOA beneficiary countries.[25] This assistance is intended to encourage governments to: (1) liberalize trade policy; (2) harmonize laws and regulations with WTO membership commitments; (3) engage in financial and fiscal restructuring; and (4) promote greater agribusiness linkages. AGOA also includes assistance for developing private sector business associations and networks among U.S. and SSA enterprises.[26] Technical assistance must be targeted to increasing the number of reverse trade missions; increasing trade in services; addressing critical agricultural policy issues; and building capabilities of African states to participate in the WTO, generally, and, particularly, in services. In FY2012, the United States reported obligating approximately $94.6 million in TCB assistance to AGOA countries, down considerably from the previous five years during which TCB funding averaged over $600 million per year.[27] Of this amount in 2012, $12.4 million was obligated for physical infrastructure development, $25.8 million on trade-related agriculture projects, and $27.7 million on competition policy, business, environment, and governance. In addition to these broad mandates, AGOA includes language pertaining to the following agencies:

- Overseas Private Investment Corporation (OPIC) – Section 123 expresses the sense of Congress that OPIC should exercise its authority to support projects in SSA and directs OPIC to increase funds directed to SSA countries.
- Export-Import Bank (Ex-Im Bank) – Section 124 of AGOA expresses the sense of Congress that the Ex-Im Bank should continue to expand its financial commitments to its loan guarantee and insurance programs to African countries and commends the Bank's sub-Saharan Africa Advisory Committee for its work in fostering economic cooperation between the United States and SSA. This committee's work was extended to September 30, 2014, in recent legislation reauthorizing the Ex-Im Bank (§23 of P.L. 112-122).[28]
- United States Trade Representative (USTR) – Section 117 supports the creation of an Assistant USTR for Africa to serve as the "primary point of contact in the executive branch for those persons engaged in trade between the United States and sub-Saharan Africa," and the chief adviser to the U.S. Trade Representative (USTR) on trade and

investment issues pertaining to Africa. This position previously had been established by President Clinton in 1998.

- U.S. Foreign Commercial Service (CS) – Section 125 notes that the CS presence in SSA had been reduced since the 1980s and the level of staffing in 1997 (seven officers in four countries) did not "adequately service the needs of U.S. businesses attempting to do business in sub-Saharan Africa."[29] Accordingly, the legislation required the posting of at least 20 CS officers in not less than 10 countries in SSA by December 31, 2001, "subject to the availability of appropriations."[30] According to data provided by the Department of Commerce for FY2012, there were five CS staff in Africa with three in South Africa and one each in Kenya and Nigeria.
- U.S. Agency for International Development (USAID) – Aside from Millennium Challenge Corporation (MCC) compacts that include TCB, USAID funds much of the trade capacity building efforts related to AGOA ($58 of the $94.6 million mentioned above). In 2011, the Administration announced the African Competitiveness and Trade Expansion (ACTE) initiative, a trade and investment initiative with funding of up to $30 million annually, subject to appropriations.[31] ACTE supports the three African Trade Hubs, one of USAID's most oft-cited AGOA-related projects.[32] Based in Ghana, Kenya, and Botswana, the Trade Hubs attempt to help potential exporters become globally competitive and make full use of their AGOA benefits.[33]

Annual Report to Congress

Originally, AGOA also required the President to submit an annual "comprehensive report on the trade and investment policy of the United States for sub-Saharan Africa." In a subsequent reauthorization of the AGOA trade preferences, this requirement was not extended. The most recent report was in 2008.

U.S. Imports under AGOA and GSP[34]

U.S. imports from AGOA countries represent a very small share of overall U.S. imports. In 2012, the United States imported $2,251 billion in goods, of which only $47.6 billion, or roughly 2%, came from AGOA countries. Nearly 75% of these imports ($34.9 billion) received duty-free treatment, under either AGOA or GSP, though crude oil accounts for much of this. Among non-energy U.S. imports, 38% received duty-free treatment under AGOA or GSP.[35]

Energy-related products (*e.g.*, crude oil) dominate U.S. imports from SSA under AGOA and GSP, representing 86% of such imports in 2012. Given SSA's abundant natural resources and the already low U.S. tariff on oil ($0.05-$0.10 per barrel), much of this trade would likely occur regardless of the preference program. The discussion that follows focuses on non-energy trade between the United States and SSA. (See the text box on page 11 for more information on U.S. oil imports under AGOA.)

In 2012, U.S. non-energy imports from SSA under AGOA and GSP were $4.8 billion (*Figure 1*). This represented a slight decline from the $5 billion in imports in 2011, but a more than three-fold increase (up from $1.3 billion) since 2001, the first full year of AGOA eligibility. Apparel products remain one of the largest non-oil import categories; however, these imports peaked in 2004 prior to the dismantling of the complex multilateral quota system, known as the Multifiber Agreement (MFA). The MFA limited U.S. apparel imports from certain countries, thus eliminating the extent of competition faced by AGOA apparel exporters. Though U.S. apparel imports still face relatively high tariffs, removal of these strict quantitative limitations reduced the AGOA countries' competitive advantage in producing apparel. U.S. apparel imports under AGOA, though very significant for some AGOA countries, represent only 1% of overall U.S. apparel imports. U.S. apparel imports totaled $77.7 billion in 2012 with $29.6 billion from China, $7.0 billion from Vietnam, and less than $1 billion total from AGOA beneficiaries (Table 1).

Table 1. U.S. Imports of Apparel Products by Country (in millions of U.S. dollars, 2012)

Top Overall Countries	Import Value	Top AGOA Countries	Import Value
China	$29,602	Lesotho	$301
Vietnam	7,009	Kenya	254
Indonesia	4,954	Mauritius	163
Bangladesh	4,322	Swaziland	60
Mexico	3,844	Botswana	11

Source: Analysis by CRS. Data from U.S. ITC.

Notes: Apparel products defined as Harmonized Tariff Schedule (HTS) chapters 61 and 62.

(in millions of U.S. dollars)

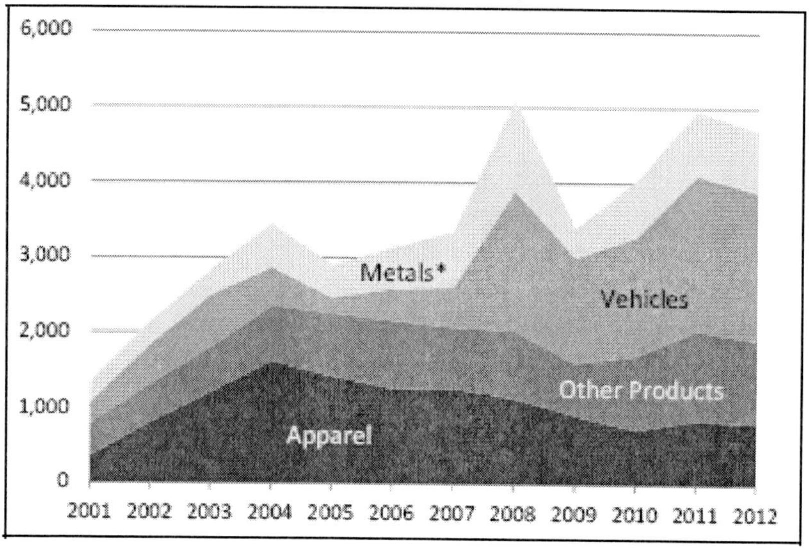

Source: Analysis by CRS. Data from U.S. International Trade Commission (ITC).
Notes: (*) Includes aluminum, iron, and steel products.

Figure 1. U.S. Imports from SSA under AGOA and GSP, excluding Crude Oil.

While U.S. apparel imports from AGOA countries have declined from their peak in 2004, imports of other products have been rising rapidly. Vehicle imports have seen strong growth, rising from $289 million in 2001 to nearly $2 billion in 2012. These and other more advanced manufactured products, such as chemicals, come almost exclusively from South Africa. Imports of products with more widespread origins have also grown, though on a more modest scale. U.S. imports of food and agriculture products, including nuts, fruits, cocoa, sugar, beverages, and tobacco have increased from $136 million to $508 million during the same period.

U.S. imports from SSA under AGOA and GSP are heavily concentrated in a few countries. *Figure 2* highlights the top exporters of non-energy products to the United States under both programs. U.S. preferential imports from South Africa totaled $3.7 billion in 2012, accounting for roughly three-quarters of all U.S. imports from SSA under AGOA/GSP. Other top exporters under AGOA/GSP are the major apparel producers: Lesotho ($301 million); Kenya ($293 million); and Mauritius ($175 million). Cote d'Ivoire was the fifth largest exporter under these preference programs, exporting largely cocoa products ($96 million). Aside from these top countries, however, the preferences are not heavily utilized. U.S. preferential imports were less than $1 million for over half of the 39 AGOA beneficiary countries in 2012.

(2012, in millions of U.S. dollars)

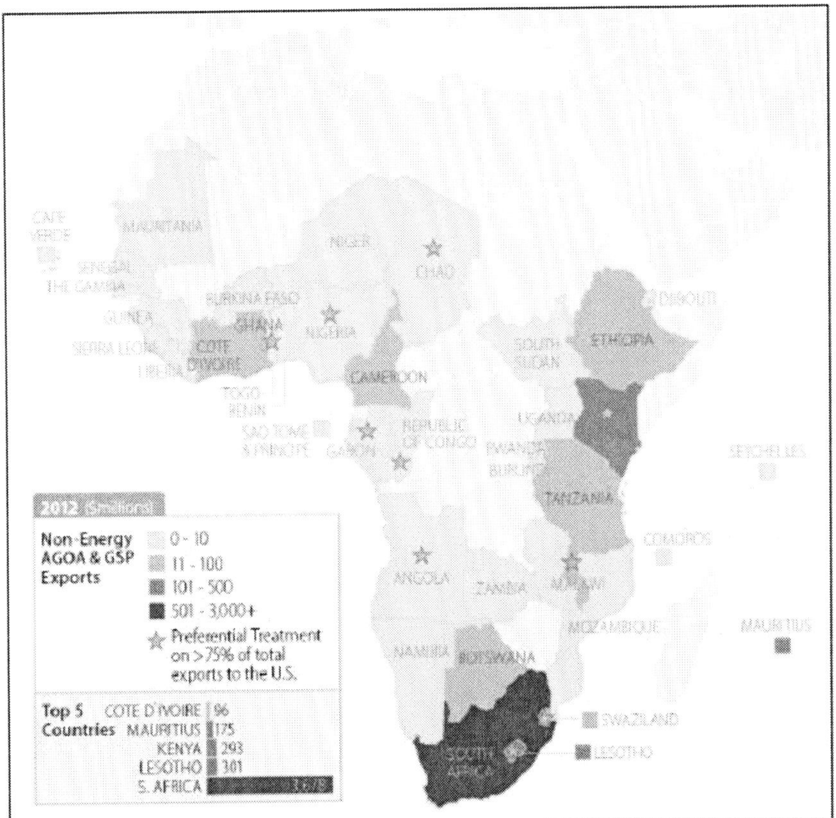

Source: Analysis by CRS. Data from U.S. ITC.

Figure 2. Top AGOA and GSP Exporters, excluding Crude Oil.

U.S. Oil Imports Under AGOA and GSP

Crude oil has been the top U.S. import from SSA under AGOA and GSP since AGOA's first full year of duty-free treatment in 2001 (Figure 3), The following are key facts regarding U.S. oil imports under AGOA and GSP.

- The top 5 AGOA-eligible oil exporters are Nigeria, Angola, Chad, Gabon, and Republic of Congo.
- Both AGOA and GSP grant duty-free status to U.S. crude oil imports.
- GSP only affords this treatment to least-developed countries (LDCs).
- Nigeria is not considered an LDC under GSP and so depends on AGOA for duty-free treatment of its crude oil exports to the United States. It is the only major AGOA-eligible oil exporter that is not considered an LDC under GSP.
- Crude oil prices have exceeded $100 a barrel in recent years. This high market value coupled with a very low U.S. import tariff, $0.05-$0.10 per barrel, makes AGOA and GSP's crude oil tariff benefit relatively insignificant.
- U.S. crude oil imports from SSA dropped 40% in 2012, which may be partially due to the increased U.S. production of shale oil, a direct competitor with oil from some SSA countries due to its similar composition.[36]

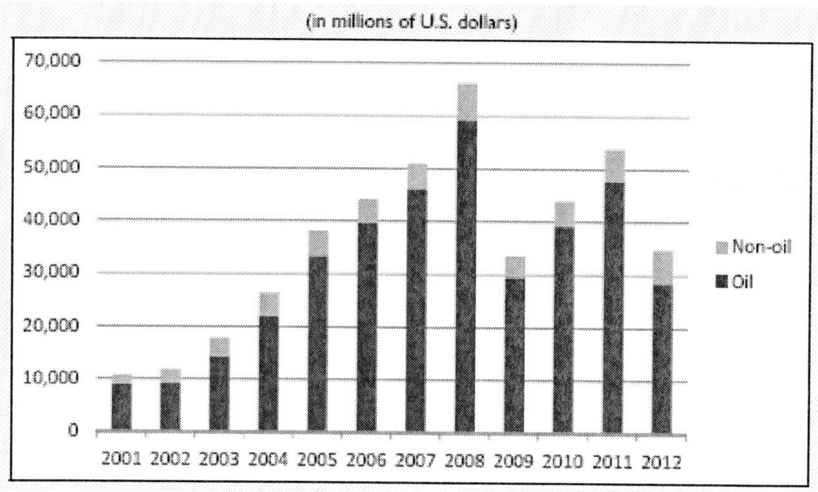

Source: Analysis by CRS. Data from U.S. ITC.

Figure 3. Oil Imports from SSA under AGOA and GSP.

IMPACTS OF AGOA

Through AGOA Congress set out to improve the economic development of SSA and increase U.S. trade ties with the region. A handful of countries have made strong use of the preference program and have increased employment in economic sectors that benefited from duty-free treatment under AGOA. For example, the government of Lesotho, one of the major apparel exporters under AGOA, estimates that employment in manufacturing rose from 19,000 in 1999 to 45,700 in June 2011.[37] A peer-reviewed economic study found a direct link between the AGOA preferences and increased U.S. imports from beneficiary countries, and concluded that these increased SSA exports were not merely diverted from other potential export destinations (*e.g.,* the European Union).[38] This relationship was strongest for the apparel sector and other sectors with high U.S. import tariffs.

Despite these achievements, challenges remain, such as the limited number of countries making significant use of the preferences, and doubts as to whether AGOA countries have been able to translate these short-term preference benefits into transformative changes in their manufacturing capabilities and overall competitiveness.[39] As highlighted above, the majority of AGOA non-oil imports come from South Africa. Among the other countries that have made significant use of the preferences, apparel exports account for most of their AGOA exports. While the apparel sector has been acknowledged as a potential launching point for more advanced manufacturing industries, the manufacturing sectors in many AGOA beneficiary countries remain highly underdeveloped. One study asserts that AGOA apparel production is concentrated in the lowest-skill tasks with little knowledge transfer to local workers and that the global competitiveness of AGOA exporters still depends on their preferential treatment.[40]

In addition to AGOA's tangible goals related to economic development and trade, AGOA also supports the achievement of other strategic objectives. AGOA serves as a focal point for U.S. economic relations with SSA. If the recent period of high economic growth in much of SSA continues, the United States may have an increasing interest in the region's potential as a consumer market and destination for both U.S. exports and foreign direct investment (FDI). A study by McKinsey estimated that the number of African households making above $5,000 per year, the point where discretionary spending begins, would rise from 85 million in 2008 to 128 million in 2020.[41] Though AGOA focuses specifically on U.S. imports, it spurs dialogue between the United

States and SSA countries on two-way trade and investment issues through the annual AGOA Forum. Through the eligibility criteria required for the program, the United States maintains some influence over the political and economic structure of the beneficiary countries. These strategic aspects of AGOA may become more important as other foreign countries, such as China, continue to increase their commercial and political ties with SSA.

REAUTHORIZATION DEBATE

AGOA's authorization is set to expire on September 30, 2015. President Obama,[42] some Members of Congress, officials from beneficiary countries, and various stakeholders have expressed an interest in renewing the preferences. Some observers have also argued that this potential reauthorization provides an opportunity to improve AGOA, addressing some of its challenges and making it more compatible with the changing economic landscape in SSA. The following are some issues that may merit consideration during AGOA's reauthorization debate.

- Investor Uncertainty, Country Eligibility, and Length of Reauthorization – Private sector actors have argued that uncertainty regarding the duration of AGOA preferences, both due to the eligibility reviews and periodic reauthorizations, hinders investment in the region. Some have called for a longer and uniform reauthorization (i.e., ten years) for all AGOA preferences, including the "third-country fabric provision," and for more transparency and greater consideration of economic implications during annual eligibility reviews.[43] On the other hand, changes to the eligibility criteria could decrease the potential leverage AGOA provides to encourage economic and political reform in beneficiary countries. Lengthened periods of authorization could also limit the incentive for more advanced economies, such as South Africa, to engage in more comprehensive trade liberalization efforts.
- Intra-African Trade –Intra-African trade and economic integration have been cited as a crucial but often absent component of economic development in the region.[44] Regional integration efforts are one way to improve these intra-African trade ties, and AGOA calls for "expanding U.S. assistance to sub-Saharan Africa's regional integration efforts." In the first decade of AGOA's enactment, African

intra-regional trade stayed flat at around 10%.[45] It may be worthwhile to evaluate the impact, if any, that AGOA and corresponding U.S. development assistance has had in improving regional integration efforts and intra-African trade, and determine whether AGOA should further address these issues.[46]

- Two-way Trade – Like other U.S. preference programs, AGOA provides preferential access to the U.S. market with no reciprocal preferential U.S. access to the beneficiary countries. In light of economic improvements in the region, some observers are now calling for a greater focus on two-way trade in AGOA. This goal was included, however, in the original AGOA legislation mandating that the Administration seek out possible FTA partners among SSA nations. Subsequent negotiations with South Africa and its regional partners in SACU began in 2003, but were ultimately unsuccessful and postponed indefinitely in 2006. The European Union (EU), however, successfully concluded an Economic Partnership Agreement (EPA) providing reciprocal preferential treatment to EU exports to South Africa, though it excludes a range of products.[47] Two relevant policy questions follow: (1) is the United States willing to negotiate less comprehensive and high-standard FTAs than it normally negotiates to gain more access to emerging markets like South Africa, or are countries in the region more prepared to engage in comprehensive, reciprocal trade talks; and (2) should AGOA include its own graduation process, which, like that for GSP, removes more economically advanced countries from the preference program once they reach a certain level of economic development (e.g., GDP/capita level)?
- Country Participation – Over half of the current AGOA beneficiaries exported less than $1 million to the United States under AGOA in 2012. Many of these are LDC AGOA countries that are eligible for duty-free treatment on apparel exports and enjoy the more flexible rules of origin ("Third-Country Fabric Provision"), giving them a significant competitive advantage over other producers. A handful of AGOA countries, particularly Kenya, Lesotho, and Mauritius, provide the bulk of apparel exports under AGOA. Should factors that helped these countries successfully utilize AGOA potentially be integrated into a revised AGOA framework to help spur similar success in other AGOA LDCs?

- Trade Capacity Building (TCB) – Exporters in AGOA countries face numerous challenges. These include poor infrastructure, inadequate access to electricity, and skilled labor shortages. AGOA sets out broad aims for TCB, which are administered through different agencies, particularly USAID. Since 2001, $4 billion has been allocated to TCB funding in AGOA countries by various U.S. government agencies, particularly USAID and MCC. Yet discussions on AGOA often center on the need for more TCB funding. In 2011 GAO reported that USAID needed better evaluation of its TCB programs.[48] In addition to the effectiveness of TCB, another issue is whether a lack of TCB funding has been a major constraint in AGOA countries' ability to take advantage of the trade preferences. In 2012, TCB funding in AGOA countries dropped to $95 million from an average of $629 million over the previous five years, largely because no new MCC compacts with TCB components were initiated with an AGOA country in 2012.
- Products Covered under AGOA Preferences – AGOA and GSP provide duty-free access on U.S. imports of approximately 5,200 tariff lines, which together with the products already duty-free in the U.S. tariff schedule, grants AGOA beneficiaries duty-free access to roughly 86% of U.S. products. While a majority of products are covered under AGOA, some of the excluded products are competitively produced in AGOA countries, particularly agricultural products.[49] Though some agriculture products are included in AGOA, those subject to tariff-rate quotas (TRQs) are limited in the amount that may enter duty-free. Expanding the products covered under AGOA could allow a greater number of AGOA beneficiaries to make use of the trade preference program. Such a move, however, could prove politically sensitive in the United States, as most items excluded from U.S. preference programs are potentially import sensitive. AGOA exporters may also have difficulty meeting U.S. food safety standards for agricultural products. Expanding access to the U.S. agriculture market may also require additional TCB funding.
- Duty-Free Quota-Free (DFQF) Beyond Africa – AGOA's tariff benefits, which include apparel products, are broader than those provided by GSP. Some argue, including in the context of the current WTO Doha negotiations, that broader DFQF tariff preferences should be granted to all least-developed countries, not just those in Africa.[50] LDCs throughout the world face relatively high U.S. import tariffs

given the particular items they export, such as apparel and agricultural products. For example, in 2012, U.S. import duties on products from Cambodia ($452 million) were higher than those from the United Kingdom ($440 million).[51] Providing broader DFQF access to LDCs would erode some of the competitive advantage AGOA apparel producers currently receive. A recent study estimates that apparel exports from AGOA countries would fall considerably if AGOA-like benefits were expanded to all LDCs.[52] Other studies, however, estimate that a broader DFQF program could actually benefit AGOA LDCs by including protected sectors such as agriculture, despite potential losses in apparel production.[53] In addition, proponents of DFQF argue that apparel products currently produced in AGOA countries could be targeted for exemption from a broader DFQF program.[54]

APPENDIX A. AGOA BENEFICIARIES

Table A-1. AGOA and GSP Eligibility, U.S. Imports, and GSP/Capita, by Country

Countries	GSP	GSP-Least Developed	AGOA	AGOA-Third Country Fabric Provision	U.S. Non-Energy Imports under AGOA/GSP (thousand $'s, 2012)	GDP/Capita ($'s, 2012)
Angola	√	√	√	√	0	5,485
Benin	√	√	√	√	49	752
Botswana	√		√		12,184	7,191
Burkina Faso	√	√	√	√	71	634
Burundi	√	√	√		18	251
Cameroon	√		√	√	33,031	1,151
Cape Verde	√		√	√	120	3,838
Central African					NA	
Republic	√	√				473
Chad	√	√	√	√	0	885
Comoros	√	√	√		0	831
Democratic					NA	
Republic of Congo	√	√				272
Republic of Congo	√		√		89	3,154

Table A-1. (Continued)

Countries	GSP	GSP-Least Developed	AGOA	AGOA-Third Country Fabric Provision	U.S. Non-Energy Imports under AGOA/GSP (thousand $'s, 2012)	GDP/Capita ($'s, 2012)
Cote d'Ivoire	√		√		96,178	1,244
Djibouti	√	√	√		0	N.A.
Equatorial Guinea					NA	24,036
Eritrea	√				NA	504
Ethiopia	√	√	√	√	21,875	470
Gabon	√		√		3	11,430
Gambia	√	√	√	√	21	512
Ghana	√		√	√	47,266	1,605
Guinea	√	√	√		79	591
Guinea-Bissau	√	√			NA	539
Kenya	√		√	√	292,828	862
Lesotho	√	√	√	√	300,618	1,193
Liberia	√	√	√	√	72	422
Madagascar	√	√			NA	447
Malawi	√	√	√	√	53,131	268
Mali	√	√			NA	694
Mauritania	√	√	√		24	1,106
Mauritius	√		√	√	175,227	8,124
Mozambique	√	√	√	√	64	579
Namibia	√		√	√	1,151	5,668
Niger	√	√	√		50	383
Nigeria	√		√	√	8,273	1,555
Rwanda	√	√	√	√	377	620
Sao Tomei and Principe	√	√	√		26	1,402
Senegal	√		√	√	481	1,032
Seychelles	√		√		0	11,758
Sierra Leone	√	√	√	√	133	635
Somalia	√	√			NA	N.A
South Africa	√		√		3,678,184	7,508
South Sudan	√	√	√		0	862
Sudan					NA	1,580
Swaziland	√		√	√	62,707	3,044
Tanzania	√	√	√	√	11,846	609
Togo	√	√	√		76	574

Countries	GSP	GSP-Least Developed	AGOA	AGOA-Third Country Fabric Provision	U.S. Non-Energy Imports under AGOA/GSP (thousand $'s, 2012)	GDP/Capita ($'s, 2012)
Uganda	√	√	√	√	1,838	547
Zambia	√	√	√	√	222	1,469
Zimbabwe					NA	788

Source: Analysis by CRS. Data from USTR and ITC.

End Notes

[1] Trade preference programs give non-reciprocal duty-free U.S. market access to select exports of eligible less-developed countries.

[2] Hearing Testimony by Florizelle Lizer, U.S. Congress, Senate Committee on Foreign Relations, Subcommittee on African Affairs, Economic Statecraft: Embracing Africa's Market Potential, 112th Cong., 2nd sess., June 28, 2012, S.Hrg. 112-604 (Washington: GPO, 2012), p. 12.

[3] Analysis by CRS. Data from International Monetary Fund, World Economic Outlook, April 2013.

[4] For example, in remarks leading up to President Obama's trip to Africa, USTR Michael Froman stated, "If we are to achieve sustainable development, it is our view that investment must be the driver." USTR, "Remarks by United States Trade Representative Michael Froman to the U.S. Global Leadership Coalition," press release, June 25, http://www.ustr.gov/about-us/press-office/press-releases/2013/june/remarks-united-states-trade-representative-michael-fr.

[5] For example, a bill has been introduced in the 113th Congress relating to efforts to increase U.S. exports to Africa (H.R. 1777 and S. 718) and the Administration has initiated programs such as Trade Africa, which centers on a potential trade and investment agreement with the East African Community.

[6] Some of this material was drawn from a previous CRS report by Vivian C. Jones.

[7] Apparel production is an important component of AGOA because it is seen as a manufacturing sector with relatively low technological and investment barriers to entry by newly industrializing countries and as having high job-generation potential for relatively low-skilled labor forces, both issues of relevance to many African countries.

[8] In addition to AGOA, there are four other U.S. regional preference programs that have different product coverage than GSP: the Caribbean Basin Economic Recovery Act (CBERA); the Caribbean Trade Partnership Act (CBTPA); the Andean Trade Preference Act (ATPA); and the Haitian Opportunity through Partnership Encouragement (HOPE) Act.8

[9] Observers cited several possible reasons for the unsuccessful FTA negotiations, including the capacity of SACU nations to negotiate a U.S.-style (comprehensive and high-standard) FTA, and disagreements between the parties on the scope and level of ambition of the negotiations.

[10] The AGOA trade preferences, including the portion covered by GSP, are in effect through September 2015, regardless of GSP's reauthorization.

[11] U.S. Government Accountability Office, U.S. Trade Preference Programs Provide Important Benefits, but a More Integrated Approach Would Better Ensure Programs Meet Shared Goals, GAO-08-443, March 2008, pp. 70-72.

[12] Ibid.

[13] TRQs are two-tiered tariffs. In-quota import quantities face one tariff, while above-quota import quantities face another, typically much higher, tariff.

[14] CRS Report RL33663, Generalized System of Preferences: Background and Renewal Debate, by Vivian C. Jones.

[15] §506A of P.L. 93-618, as added by §111 of P.L. 106-200, and amended by §7 of P.L. 108-274.

[16] For more information, see Department of Commerce, Office of Textiles and Apparel (OTEXA) Summary of AGOA textile and apparel provisions at OTEXA website, http://otexa.ita.doc.gov.

[17] Karina Fernandez-Stark, Stacey Frederick, and Gary Gereffi, The Apparel Global Value Chain, Duke Center on Globalization Governance and Competitiveness, November 2011.

[18] Paul Collier and Anthony Venables, Rethinking Trade Preferences to Help Diversify African Exports, Centre for Economic Policy Research, June 2007.

[19] A "yarn forward" rule means that, in order to qualify for trade benefits under an FTA, all products in a garment from the yarn stage forward must be made in one of the countries that is party to the agreement.

[20] World Trade Organization, World Tariff Profiles - United States, 2012.

[21] For a discussion of challenges faced by African firms, see Ann E. Harrison, Justin Yifu Lin, and L. Colin Xu, Explaining Africa's (Dis)Advantage, National Bureau of Economic Research, Working Paper 18683, January 2013.

[22] Department of Commerce, Office of Textiles and Apparel (OTEXA) Summary of AGOA textile and apparel provisions at OTEXA website, http://otexa.ita.doc.gov.

[23] 19 U.S.C. § 2462(a)(2) and 19 U.S.C. § 3721(c)(3).

[24] Representatives from appropriate sub-Saharan African regional organizations and government officials from other appropriate countries in sub-Saharan Africa also could be invited, and generally are. African countries hosting the Forum must be nominated by their participant peers and be able to sponsor associated costs.

[25] Section 122 of P.L. 106-200 (19 U.S.C. § 3732).

[26] Ibid.

[27] USAID, which administers the collection and dissemination of the data on TCB, includes portions of Millennium Challenge Corporation (MCC) compacts, such as infrastructure projects, in these figures. USAID reports the MCC funding in the year it is granted, though the distribution of the funds occurs over several years. No new MCC compacts with TCB components were initiated with AGOA countries in 2012, which explains the large drop in TCB funding. U.S. Agency for International Development, Trade Capacity Building Database, http://tcb.eads.usaidallnet.gov/.

[28] Export-Import Bank Reauthorization Act, 12 U.S.C. 635(b)(9)(B)(iii).

[29] AGOA, §125(a)(4).

[30] AGOA, §125(b).

[31] USAID, "U.S. Announces New African Trade Capacity Building Initiative at AGOA Forum," press release, June 9, 2011, http://www.usaid.gov/news-information/press-releases/us-announces-new-african-trade-capacity-building initiative-agoa.

[32] For example, see Hearing Testimony by Earl W. Gast, U.S. Congress, Senate Committee on Foreign Relations, Subcommittee on African Affairs, Economic Statecraft: Embracing Africa's Market Potential, 112th Cong., 2nd sess., June 28, 2012, S.Hrg. 112-604 (Washington: GPO, 2012), p. 10.

[33] Each of the three regional Trade Hubs has its own web site with information on its activities. For more information see: West Africa - http://www.watradehub.com/aboutus; East Africa - http://www.competeafrica.org/; and South Africa - http://www.satradehub.org/.

[34] AGOA and GSP overlap in their product coverage so this discussion considers them jointly. Trade data in this section come from the U.S. International Trade Commission's dataweb, http://dataweb.usitc.gov/, and http://dataweb.usitc.gov/africa/trade_data.asp.

[35] Though only 38% of non-oil imports entered the United States under AGOA or GSP, roughly 90% of non-oil imports entered duty-free, because a large portion of products face no U.S. import tariff.

[36] Sarah Kent, "Nigeria Bearing Brunt of U.S. Shale-Oil Boom," The Wall Street Journal, March 6, 2013.

[37] Central Bank of Lesotho, Africa Growth and Opportunities Act (AGOA): Economic Impact and Future Prospects, CBL Economic Review No. 131, June 2011, p. 3.

[38] Garth Frazer and Johannes Van Biesebroeck, "Trade Growth under the African Growth and Opportunity Act," The Review of Economics and Statistics, vol. 92, no. 1 (February 2010).

[39] Niall Condon and Matthew Stern, The Effectiveness of African Growth and Opportunity Act (AGOA) in Increasing Trade from Least Developed Countries, EPPI-Centre, Social Research Unit, Institute of Education, University of London, March 2011.

[40] Lawrence Edwards and Robert Z. Lawrence, AGOA Rules: The Intended and Unintended Consequences of Special Fabric Provisions, National Bureau of Economic Research, Working Paper 16623, December 2010.

[41] McKinsey Global Institute, Lions on the Move: The Progress and Potential of African Economies, June 2010, p. 22.

[42] The White House, "Remarks by President Obama at Business Leaders Forum," press release, July 1, 2013, http://www.whitehouse.gov/the-press-office/2013/07/01/remarks-president-obama-business-leaders-forum.

[43] The Corporate Council on Africa, Promoting Shared Interests: Policy Recommendations on Africa for the Second Term of the Obama Administration, April 2013, p. 18.

[44] Africa's trade with itself accounts for only 11% of its total trade, compared with 50% in developing Asia and 70% in Europe. United Nations Conference on Trade and Development, Intra-African Trade: Unlocking Private Sector Dynamism, Economic Development in Africa Report 2013, July 2013.

[45] Brookings Africa Growth Initiative, Accelerating Growth through Improved Intra-African Trade, January 2012, p. 2.

[46] The Administration recently announced the Trade Africa initiative, which centers on a new trade and investment partnership with the East African Community (EAC). This may eventually include a bilateral investment treaty (BIT) with the EAC, which would be the first such treaty with a regional group. http://www.whitehouse.gov/the-press-office/2013/07/01/fact-sheet-trade-africa.

[47] GSP already includes language related to such occurrences, declaring a country ineligible if it "affords preferential treatment to the products of a developed country, other than the United State, which has, or is likely to have, a significant adverse effect on United States commerce." 19 U.S.C. § 2462(b)(2)(C).

[48] U.S. Government Accountability Office, The United States Provides Wide-ranging Trade Capacity Building Assistance, but Better Reporting and Evaluation Are Needed, GA0-11-727, 2011, http://www.gao.gov/products/GAO11-727.

[49] GAO, Options for Congressional Consideration to Improve U.S. Trade Preference Programs, Prepared Statement for Hearing, GAO-10-262T, November 2009, p. 4.

[50] Kimberly Ann Elliott, Why Is Opening the U.S. Market to Poor Countries So Hard?, Center for Global Development, January 2012.

[51] Calculated duties according to U.S. ITC tariff and trade dataweb.

[52] Brookings and United Nations Economic Commission for Africa, The African Growth and Opportunity Act: An Empirical Analysis of the Possibilities Post-2015, July 2013, p. 17.

[53] Antoine Bouet et al., The Costs and Benefits of Duty-Free, Quota-Free Market Access for Poor Countries: Who and What Matters, Center for Global Development, Working Paper 206, March 2010.

[54] Letter from Kimberly Elliott, Center for Global Development, to Michael Froman, USTR, June 24, 2013, http://www.cgdev.org/publication/supporting-multilateralism-and-development-us-trade-policy-duty-free-quota-freemarket.

In: The African Growth and Opportunity Act ISBN: 978-1-62948-299-6
Editors: H. Sarisohn and J. Cohen

Chapter 2

U.S. TRADE AND INVESTMENT RELATIONS WITH SUB-SAHARAN AFRICA AND THE AFRICAN GROWTH AND OPPORTUNITY ACT*

Vivian C. Jones and Brock R. Williams

SUMMARY

Following the end of the apartheid era in South Africa in the early 1990s, the United States sought to increase economic relations with sub-Saharan Africa (SSA). President Clinton instituted several measures that dealt with investment, debt relief, and trade. Congress passed legislation that required the President to develop a trade and development policy for Africa.

Between 1960 and 1973, Africa's economic growth was relatively strong, followed by a period of stagnation and decline for the subsequent two decades in many SSA countries. Current perspectives, however, indicate that many of the fastest-growing countries in the world are on the African continent, and the International Monetary Fund (IMF) projects that the SSA region will grow in terms of real GDP by 5.3% in 2012 and 2013.

---

* This is an edited, reformatted and augmented version of the Congressional Research Service Publication, CRS Report for Congress RL31772, dated November 14, 2012.

In 2000, Congress approved new U.S. trade and investment legislation for SSA in the African Growth and Opportunity Act (AGOA; Title I, P.L. 106-200). According to U.S. trade statistics, U.S. trade with SSA has comprised 1% to 2% of U.S. total trade with the world. AGOA extends preferential treatment to U.S. imports from eligible countries that are pursuing market reform measures. Data show that U.S. imports under AGOA are mostly energy products, but imports of other products have grown significantly. AGOA mandated that U.S. officials meet regularly with their counterparts in SSA, and 11 of these meetings have been held to date. The 11th AGOA Forum was held from June 14 to June 15, 2012, in Washington, DC.

AGOA also directed the President to provide U.S. government technical assistance and trade capacity support to AGOA beneficiary countries. Government agencies that have roles in this effort include the U.S. Agency for International Development, the Assistant U.S. Trade Representative for Africa (established by statute under AGOA), the Overseas Private Investment Corporation, the Export-Import Bank, the U.S. and Foreign Commercial Service, and the Trade and Development Agency. In AGOA, Congress declared that free-trade agreements should be negotiated, where feasible, with interested SSA countries. Related to this provision, negotiations on a free-trade agreement with the Southern African Customs Union (SACU), which includes South Africa and four other countries, began in June 2003, but were suspended in April 2006.

The 112th Congress enacted legislation to extend through September 2015 an expiring provision in AGOA, which allows apparel made in lesser-developed countries to be made of yarns and fabrics from any country and still receive duty-free treatment, subject to a cap (P.L. 112-163). This amendment to AGOA also added South Sudan to the list of SSA countries eligible for AGOA benefits. Eligible countries may become AGOA beneficiaries subject to approval by the Administration.

Legislation is pending to further enhance U.S.-SSA trade relations. H.R. 4221 and S. 2215 seek to increase U.S. exports to Africa, in part, through strategies aimed at further developing relationships between the United States and African countries on a government-to-government level, fostering private sector U.S.-African ties, and targeting more U.S. export financing toward trade with Africa. An amended version of S. 2215 was ordered reported by the Senate Foreign Relations Committee in September 2012. H.R. 656, a separate initiative, would create at the State Department a Special Representative for United States-Africa Trade, Development, and Diaspora Affairs that would also promote U.S. trade and investment ties with SSA.

INTRODUCTION

A key element in U.S. policy toward Africa is the potential benefit from increased trade and commercial ties between the United States and Africa.[1] Interest in increasing bilateral commerce began after the end of the apartheid era in South Africa in the early 1990s. In 1993, Congress approved the end of anti-apartheid restrictions, and later that year then-Commerce Secretary Ron Brown led a business delegation to South Africa. In subsequent years, the Administration has also instituted several measures to help sub-Saharan African (SSA) countries and increase U.S. trade and investment in the region.

At the same time, Congress developed legislation that sought to improve U.S.-Africa trade relations. In the 1994 legislation to implement the Uruguay Round of multilateral trade agreements (P.L. 103-465), Congress directed the President to develop and implement a comprehensive trade and development policy for the countries of Africa, and subsequently introduced legislation to authorize a new trade and investment policy for sub-Saharan Africa. In 2000, Congress approved the African Growth and Opportunity Act (AGOA; Title I, P.L. 106-200). AGOA offers trade preferences and other economic benefits to SSA countries that meet certain criteria, including progress towards a market economy, respect for the rule of law, and human and worker rights. In AGOA, Congress also declared that free-trade agreements should also be negotiated, where feasible, with interested SSA countries.

AGOA has been amended several times since its initial enactment. In 2002, Congress amended AGOA to further increase market access for products from SSA.[2] In 2004, Congress passed legislation to extend AGOA benefits beyond the original deadline and to clarify certain provisions. This legislation also included directives to the President on investment initiatives and technical assistance. Congress passed legislation in 2006 to further amend AGOA and extend certain provisions concerning textile and apparel imports to 2012.[3] One of these provisions, the "third-country fabric provision," permits imports, subject to a cap, of apparel made in designated lesser-developed SSA countries of third-country yarns and fabrics (meaning that the yarns and fabrics may come from any country). This provision was recently extended through September 2015.[4]

This report examines African economic trends and U.S. trade and investment flows with SSA. It discusses the provisions of AGOA and the changes that have occurred since its enactment. It concludes with a brief discussion of issues for Congress.

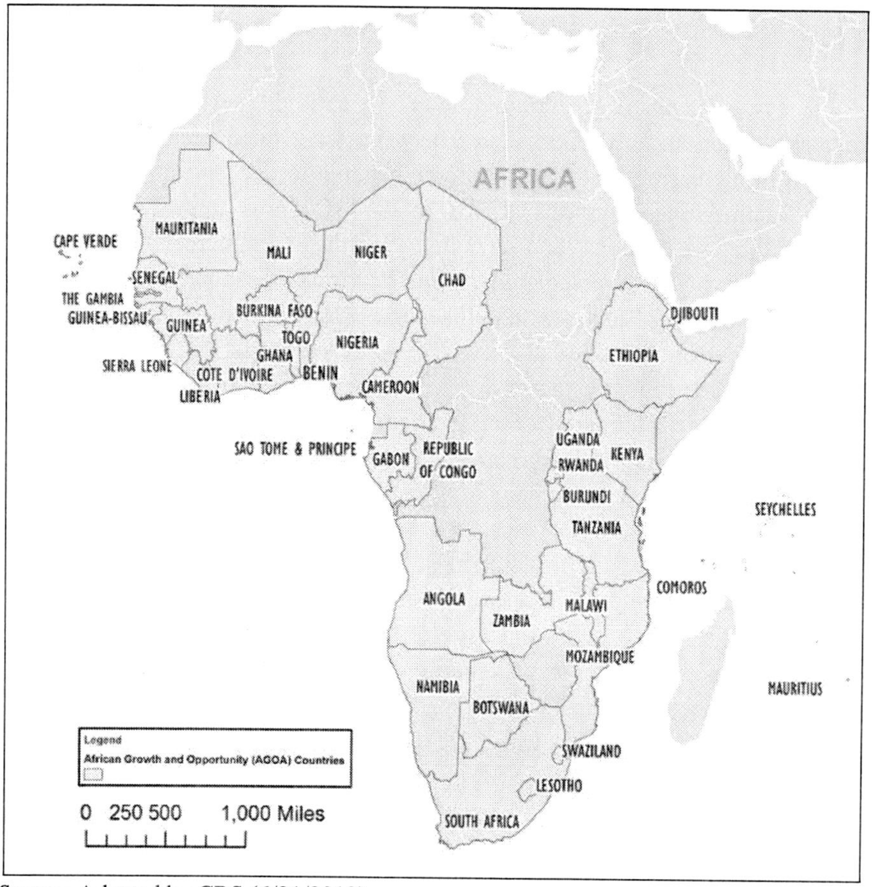

Source: Adapted by CRS (6/21/2012).

Figure 1. African Countries and AGOA Eligibility Status, 2012.

PERSPECTIVES ON THE SUB-SAHARAN AFRICAN ECONOMY

Historical Perspectives

The historical pattern of contemporary Africa's economic growth provides insights to help understand Africa's current economic situation and policy options. Between 1960 and 1973, which is the period immediately following independence in most African countries, economic growth was reasonably strong in many SSA countries. Most African countries experienced a sharp decline in their growth trends at some point between 1973 and 1980, followed by persistent stagnation until the early 1990s. Average SSA per-capita GDP (PPP data) reached its minimum point in the mid-1990s, and still had not recovered to 1970s levels in 2005.[5] Another factor that characterized growth in many African countries—and in many cases continues to affect economic development patterns—is high economic growth volatility, a common feature in SSA countries' historical trends. A 2007 World Bank study found that SSA has experienced more growth volatility than other regions, resulting in dampened investments and obscuring periods of good performance for some countries. The report found that this volatility has been caused by conflict, poor governance, and fluctuating world commodity prices. The authors of the study contend that reducing volatility is at least as important as promoting growth.[6] In the 1990s, many African countries made a modest recovery until about 1994, but the growth rates for the remainder of the period tended to remain far below the first post-colonial phase.[7]

The causes of this period of slow economic growth in the region have been a source of debate among development economists. Analysts have cited poor governance, political instability, geographic features, and historical conditions such as colonialism as different reasons for Africa's economic malaise. Other factors cited included slow accumulation of both human and physical capital, dependence on single commodity exports, low productivity growth and pressures from high population growth rates, and high dependence on foreign aid.

Following this period of stagnation, the past decade has seen considerable improvements in governance and economic growth in many parts of Africa, although many countries continue to experience political instability, poor economic performance, and lack of progress in improving social welfare indicators. Poverty and inequitable income distribution also remain common in many countries. Despite these challenges, many countries are experiencing rapid economic growth.

Current Perspectives

The International Monetary Fund (IMF) projects that the SSA region will grow in terms of real GDP by 5.3% in 2012 and 2013 (see **Table 1**).[8] These projections, however, mask significant disparities among the 44 countries the IMF considers in its regional analysis. For example, in its *Regional Economic*

Outlook, released in October 2012, the IMF projected that oil-exporting countries in SSA would experience average real GDP growth of 6.7% in 2012, and 6.0% in 2013. Relatively stable, low-income, non-energy-producing countries (such as Ethiopia, Burkina Faso, and Kenya) are expected to grow on average by 5.9% in 2012 and 6.1% in 2013, while middle income countries (such as South Africa) are projected to grow by 3.4% in 2012 and 3.8% in 2013. The IMF also projects that more than half of the 12 SSA countries identified as "fragile" countries, due to prolonged institutional weakness or conflict (such as the Democratic Republic of Congo, Guinea, and Liberia), are expected to see stronger or stable growth in 2012 (6.6%) and 2013 (5.8%).[9] This improved economic performance may reflect many factors, including better governance, increased trade flows, strong commodity prices, rising aid flows, and debt forgiveness.[10] Rising incomes and expanding urban middle classes in some countries, economic diversification, increased access to communications technologies, and multiple other factors could also contribute to such trends.

Table 1. Real GDP Growth in sub-Saharan Africa (percent change)

Country Group	2004-2008 (average)	2009	2010	2011	2012 (projected)	2013 (projected)
Oil Exporters	8.6	5.1	6.6	6.3	6.7	6.0
Middle Income	5.0	-0.6	3.8	4.5	3.4	3.8
Low Income	7.3	5.4	6.4	5.5	5.9	6.1
Fragile	2.5	3.1	4.2	2.3	6.6	6.5
Total SSA	6.5	2.8	5.3	5.2	5.3	5.3
World	4.6	-0.6	5.1	3.8	3.3	3.6

Source: International Monetary Fund, Regional Economic Outlook, sub-Saharan Africa, October 2012.

Notes: IMF Country Groupings: **Oil Exporting Countries:** Angola, Cameroon, Chad, Equatorial Guinea, Gabon, Nigeria, Republic of Congo. **Middle Income Countries:** Botswana, Cape Verde, Ghana, Lesotho, Mauritius, Namibia, Senegal, Seychelles, South Africa, Swaziland, Zambia. **Non-Fragile Low Income Countries:** Benin, Burkina Faso, Ethiopia, the Gambia, Kenya, Madagascar, Mali, Mozambique, Niger, Rwanda, Sierra Leone, Tanzania, Uganda. **Fragile Countries:** Burundi, Central African Republic, Comoros, Democratic Republic of the Congo, Cote d'Ivoire, Eritrea, Guinea, Guinea-Bissau, Liberia, Sao Tome and Principe, Togo, Zimbabwe.

U.S. foreign direct investment (FDI) flows to the region in 2011 amounted to about \$3.1 billion, with South Africa (\$722 million), Angola (\$707 million), Ghana (\$250 million), and Liberia (\$113 million) as the major destinations of those investment flows.[11] According to United Nations (UN) data, total world FDI to SSA amounted to about \$35 billion in 2011.[12] Leading SSA country destinations for worldwide direct investment in 2011 included Nigeria (\$8.9 billion), South Africa (\$5.8 billion), and Ghana (\$3.2 billion).

Investment and Growth Challenges

Despite improved economic performance in many African countries in recent years, the economic challenges facing Africa remain significant. African countries are vulnerable to volatile weather conditions, commodity price fluctuations, and poor road and other infrastructure conditions, as well as ongoing political instability in parts of the continent. Many countries have also faced difficulties in reducing high rates of poverty, improving social welfare indicators, combating corruption, and diversifying their economies. In addition, limited integration of regional trade regimes and transport systems often inhibits intra-regional trade, as well as foreign investment. Many countries' domestic market demand is not large enough to draw the attention of large foreign and U.S. firms, which may prefer to deal with larger regional markets.[13]

Much of sub-Saharan Africa's trade with the world is largely still based on primary product exports, such as oil and other mineral fuels (about 54% of its exports to the world by value in 2010); precious stones and metals (10%); and ores, slag, and ash (5%).[14] As a result, many sub- Saharan African countries continue to be vulnerable—as do many developing countries and regions—to the rise and fall of international commodity prices.

HIV/AIDS and Other Health Challenges

The HIV/AIDS pandemic is also straining some African economies and threatens to curtail future economic growth. SSA is the region most affected by HIV/AIDS. As of 2010, an estimated 22.9 million people were living with HIV-AIDS in SSA, accounting for 68% of all people living with HIV worldwide. Nine countries with the world's highest HIV prevalence rates worldwide are located in Southern Africa, where an estimated 11.1 million people were living with HIV in 2010. Swaziland has the world's highest prevalence rate (25.9%), and South Africa has the world's largest HIV-positive population (5.6 million).[15] In 2010, about 1.9 million people in SSA contracted HIV and approximately 1.2 million people in the region died from AIDS.[16] The pandemic not only diverts resources from investments in productive resources to social services to care for the sick and dying, but it also erodes human capital by striking some of the most productive members of society: skilled workers, teachers, and professionals.[17]

Africa also suffers disproportionately high disease burdens attributable to such illnesses as malaria, tuberculosis and other respiratory diseases, and water-born diarrheal infections, and many countries face severe health care delivery system constraints.[18]

Foreign Debt Burden

The debt burden carried by SSA countries has been identified as a drag on the economies of the region. In 2010, the states of SSA owed foreign creditors an estimated total of $143 billion.[19] SSA's total government debt as a percentage of GDP averaged 33.1% in 2011 (see **Table 3**).[20] Declines in some SSA countries' external debt are due to ongoing comprehensive debt relief initiatives begun in 1996, including the Heavily Indebted Poor Countries Initiative (HIPC), the Multilateral Debt Relief Initiative (MDRI), and the Paris Club agreement with Nigeria.[21]

Table 2. SSA Countries with Highest Estimated Adult (15-49) HIV Prevalence Rate (Percentage), 2009

Country	Estimate (%)
Swaziland	25.9
Botswana	24.8
Lesotho	23.6
South Africa	17.8
Zimbabwe	14.3
Zambia	13.5
Namibia	13.1
Mozambique	11.5
Malawi	11.0
Kenya	6.3
SSA Average	5.9

Source: UNAIDS Report on the Global AIDS Epidemic, 2010.

Table 3. SSA Government Debt (as percent of GDP)

Country Grouping	2004 – 2008 (average)	2009	2010	2011
Oil Exporters	29.4	21.8	20.5	20.5
Middle Income	32.6	31.5	34.9	37.8
Low Income	50.6	34.8	37.2	37.3
Fragile	112.5	88.8	58.3	65.1
Total SSA	38.7	32.3	31.5	33.1

Source: International Monetary Fund, Regional Economic Outlook, sub-Saharan Africa, October 2012.

Notes: IMF Country Groupings: **Oil Exporting Countries:** Angola, Cameroon, Chad, Equatorial Guinea, Gabon, Nigeria, Republic of Congo. **Middle Income Countries:** Botswana, Cape Verde, Ghana, Lesotho, Mauritius, Namibia, Senegal, Seychelles, South Africa, Swaziland, Zambia. **Non-Fragile Low Income Countries:** Benin, Burkina Faso, Ethiopia, the Gambia, Kenya, Madagascar, Mali, Mozambique, Niger, Rwanda, Sierra Leone, Tanzania, Uganda. **Fragile Countries:** Burundi, Central African Republic, Comoros, Democratic Republic of the Congo, Cote d'Ivoire, Eritrea, Guinea, Guinea-Bissau, Liberia, Sao Tome and Principe, Togo, Zimbabwe.

U.S.-Africa Trade and Investment Trends

U.S. Trade with sub-Saharan Africa

U.S. imports from SSA countries fell in 2008 and 2009, possibly due to the spillover effects of the global financial crisis and falling demand.[22] According to the IMF, however, the SSA region is currently showing solid macroeconomic performance, and economic activity had expanded strongly in 2010 through 2012 to date.[23] This is illustrated, in part, by an expansion in total U.S. trade (imports plus exports) with SSA countries in 2010 and 2011, which grew by 29.5% and 17% respectively, after a decrease in total trade by 40% in the 2008-2009 time frame (see **Table 4**), as well as a continuing large increase in trade with China.

The United States conducts a small share of its total trade with SSA countries. In 2011, the United States imported $74 billion from SSA countries, or about 3.4% of total U.S. global imports of $2.2 trillion. The United States exported $20.3 billion to the region in 2011, or 1.5% of total U.S. exports of $1.3 trillion. Nevertheless, total trade (exports plus imports) between the

United States and sub-Saharan Africa grew 51% between 2009 and 2011, up from $62.4 billion in 2009 to $94.3 billion in 2011 (see **Table 4**). Certain external factors, including increases in oil and other prices for natural resources, may also account, in part, for the dramatic growth (by value) in U.S.- SSA trade.

COMPARING CHINESE AND U.S. TRADE WITH AFRICA[24]

The value of total trade between China and Africa stood at $8.9 billion in the year 2000. In 2009, Chinese-African trade, totaling $70.4 billion, surpassed that of U.S.-Africa trade ($62 billion), and reached $127.3 billion in 2011, an increase of 1,423% over the 2000 level.[25] Africa's share of global Chinese trade also grew over the past decade, from 1.9% of Chinese global trade in 2000 to 3.5% of China's global trade in 2011. China is also Africa's largest single source of imports, while the United States is its largest export destination. In 2011, about 62% of African exports to China consisted of crude oil (over $24.77 billion of which came from Angola, the source of over 9% of China's oil imports in 2011). Another 34% was made up of raw materials, mostly metal commodities and wood. Oil also dominates Africa's exports to the United States; crude oil made up about 75% of U.S. imports from Africa in 2011. Both China and the United States export a highly diverse, variable array of products to Africa, notably equipment, machinery, vehicles, and other technology. U.S.-African trade has also grown over the past decade, but not as rapidly as Sino-African trade.[26]

A significant portion of U.S. trade with sub-Saharan Africa is with a small number of countries. About 79% of U.S. imports from the region were from three SSA countries in 2011: Nigeria (47%), Angola (19%), and South Africa (13%). Exports were similarly concentrated, with three countries receiving 68%: South Africa (34%), Nigeria (22%), and Angola (12%). All other countries accounted for less than 6% each of U.S. imports from the region (see **Figure 3**).

Natural resources continue to dominate U.S. imports from SSA. The leading U.S. imports from SSA in 2011 were mineral fuels and mineral oils ($58.97 billion, see **Table 5**). Nigeria was the greatest source of U.S. oil imports and was the fifth-largest global supplier (by value) of U.S. oil imports (of a total of $454 billion worldwide).[27] In 2011, Nigeria supplied 56% of U.S. petroleum imports from SSA, which accounted for about 7.4% of global U.S. oil imports. Angola supplied another 23% of U.S. petroleum from the region, Chad supplied 5%, and Congo (ROC) supplied 4%.[28]

Table 4. U.S. Goods Trade with SSA Countries (in $ billions)

Trade Flow	2008	2009	2010	2011	Percentage Change 2010 and 2011 (%)
Total U.S. Exports	18.0	14.6	16.4	20.3	24%
Total U.S. Imports	86.1	47.9	64.4	74.0	15%
Total Trade (Imports + Exports)	104.1	62.4	80.8	94.3	17%
Imports under AGOA (includes GSP)	*65.1*	*33.5*	*43.9*	*53.8*	*23%*

Source: U.S. International Trade Commission Trade Dataweb, http://dataweb.usitc.gov.

Notes: Domestic Exports, FAS value; Imports for Consumption, Customs Value. Total Imports under AGOA is a subset of total U.S. imports from SSA countries.

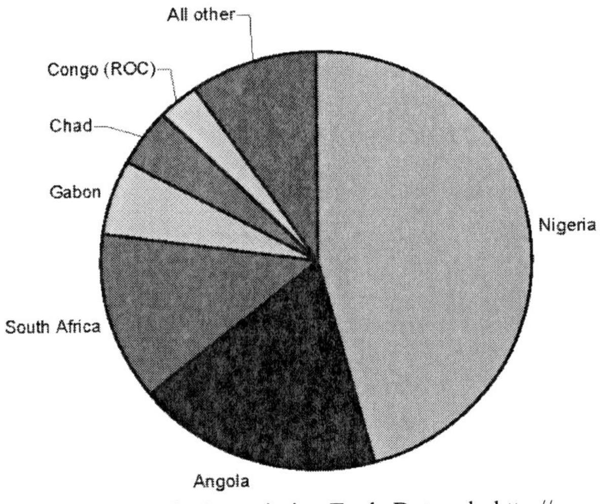

Source: U.S. International Trade Commission Trade Dataweb, http://www.usitc.gov.

Figure 2. U.S. Imports from sub-Saharan Africa by Country, 2011.

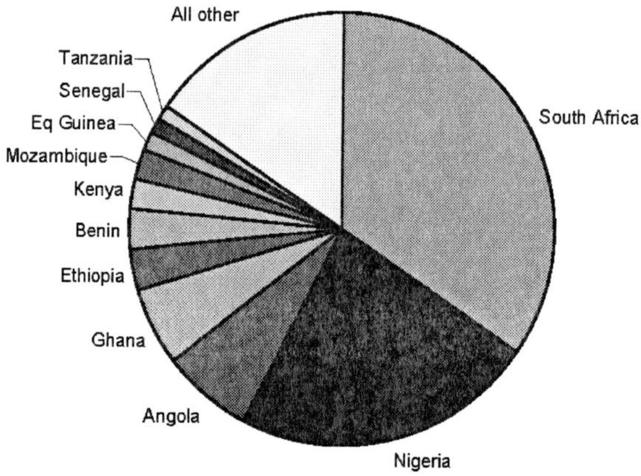

Source: U.S. International Trade Commission Trade Dataweb, http://dataweb.usitc.gov.

Figure 3. U.S. Exports to sub-Saharan Africa by Country, 2011.

Table 5. Top Ten U.S. Imports from sub-Saharan Africa, 2010 and 2011 (in $ billions)

HTS Number	2010	2011	Percent Change 2010-2011
27-Mineral fuels and oil	51.38	58.97	14.80%
71-Pearls, Precious Stones, Precious Metals, etc., Coin	3.95	4.33	9.80%
87-Vehicles, Except Railway Or Tramway, And Parts	1.61	2.16	34.10%
18-Cocoa and cocoa preparations	1.04	1.27	22.60%
29-Organic chemicals	1.22	1.16	-4.70%
72-Iron and steel	0.76	0.89	16.70%
26-Ores, slag, and ash	0.67	0.79	17.70%
62-Articles of apparel and clothing accessories, not knitted or crocheted	0.40	0.46	14.70%
84-Nuclear Reactors, Boilers, Machinery and Parts	0.36	0.46	26.30%
61-Articles of apparel and clothing accessories, knitted or crocheted	0.39	0.44	14.30%
Subtotal	61.77	70.94	14.80%
All Other	2.58	3.08	19.40%
Total	64.35	74.02	15.00%

Source: U.S. International Trade Commission Trade Dataweb, http://www.usitc.gov.
Note: U.S. Imports for Consumption.

Precious stones and metals were another major U.S. import from SSA in 2011.[29] South Africa led this category (imports included platinum, diamonds, other semi-precious stones, and coins) with about $4.2 billion in U.S. imports; followed by Botswana, Angola, and Namibia—all diamond producers—at about $275 million, $169 million, and $100 million, respectively (see **Table 5** and **Figure 4**).[30]

Although natural resources are the major category of U.S. imports from SSA countries, there have also been marked increases in imports of other products, including textiles and apparel, vehicle parts and transportation equipment, and agricultural products. A 2009 report by the U.S. International Trade Commission (USITC) indicated that certain SSA countries have the potential to competitively produce certain textile and apparel inputs. Since cotton is the primary fiber currently used in the production of yarn and fabric in SSA countries, and is grown in large quantities in the region, the USITC found that cotton products seem to have the most competitive potential. The report also stated that certain niche apparel products manufactured in small quantities could also be successful in the U.S. market, including organic cotton products; yarn and knit fabric of modal and other specialty manmade fibers; hand-loomed fabric of cotton and silk for home furnishings and apparel; African print fabrics; and zippers and ornamental trim products.[31]

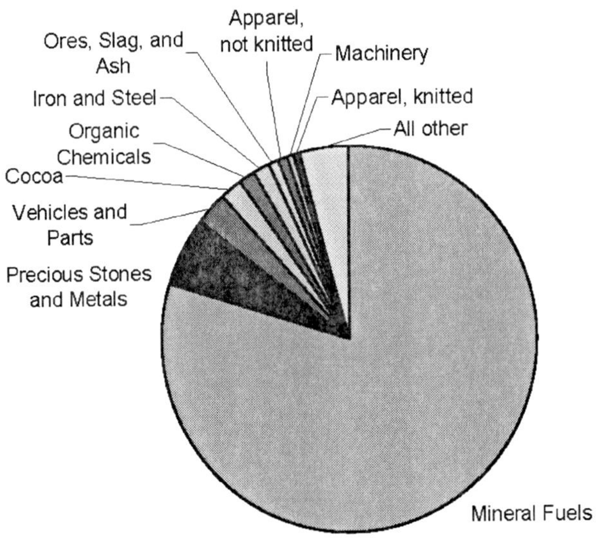

Source: U.S. International Trade Commission Trade Dataweb, http://www.usitc.gov.

Figure 4. U.S. Imports from sub-Saharan Africa by Product Category, 2011.

Table 6. Top Ten U.S. Exports to sub-Saharan Africa (in $ billions)

HTS Number	2010	2011	Percent Change
84-Nuclear Reactors, Boilers, Machinery and Parts	3.43	3.93	14.30%
87-Vehicles, Except Railway Or Tramway, And Parts	2.40	3.45	43.60%
27-Mineral Fuels and Oil	1.41	1.84	30.30%
10-Cereals	1.36	1.79	31.60%
88-Aircraft, Spacecraft, and Parts	1.11	1.51	35.70%
85-Electric Machinery; Sound and TV Equipment and Parts	0.81	0.75	-7.70%
98-Special Classification Provisions	0.60	0.72	18.50%
71-Pearls, Precious Stones, Precious Metals, etc., Coin	0.42	0.62	44.90%
90-Optical, Photography, Medical or Surgical Instruments	0.60	0.58	-3.50%
39-Plastics and Articles Thereof	0.47	0.56	20.40%
Subtotal	12.63	15.73	24.60%
All Other	3.81	4.57	19.80%
Total	16.44	20.30	23.50%

Source: U.S. International Trade Commission Trade Dataweb, http://www.usitc.gov

U.S. exports to sub-Saharan Africa were more diverse. Machinery and parts was the leading export sector in 2011 (22% of U.S. exports to the region), followed by transportation equipment (17%), cereals (8%), mineral fuels (8%), aircraft and parts (7%), and electrical machinery (6%) (see **Figure 5**).

U.S. Investment in sub-Saharan Africa

U.S. foreign direct investment (FDI) in Africa is characterized by the following:

- SSA countries are a relatively minor destination of U.S. FDI. Africa, as a whole, hosts about 1% of total U.S. FDI (see **Figure 6**).[32]

- U.S. FDI in Africa is largely concentrated in mining and extractive industries, which together comprise some \$33 billion of the \$57 billion total stock of U.S. FDI in Africa (see **Figure 7**).[33]
- U.S. FDI in African manufacturing industries has mostly been directed toward South Africa, which has received about 67% of total U.S. FDI in Africa's manufacturing sector.[34]

In 2011, the latest year for which annual investment data are available, outflows of U.S. FDI abroad to SSA (\$3.4 billion) were only about one-third greater than inflows of FDI into the United States from SSA (\$2.1 billion). The three countries in SSA with the largest stock of U.S. FDI in 2011 were Mauritius, South Africa, and Angola (stock column, **Table 7**). This stock of FDI represents an accumulation over time. In terms of one-year flows for 2011, the top recipients were South Africa, Angola, and Ghana (see flow column).

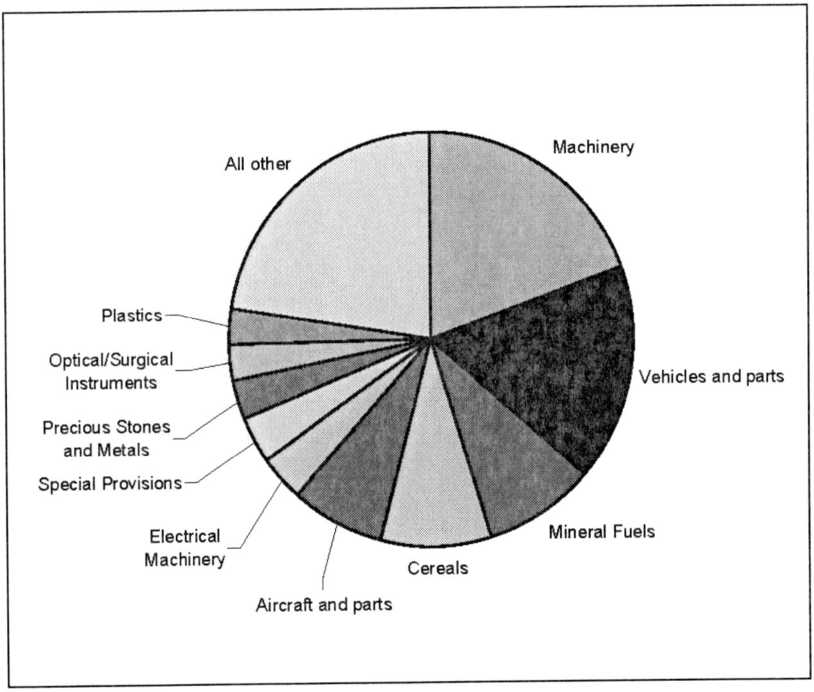

Source: U.S. International Trade Commission Trade Dataweb, http://www.usitc.gov.

Figure 5. U.S. Exports to sub-Saharan Africa by Product Category, 2011.

Table 7. Major Destinations of U.S. Foreign Direct Investment (FDI) in SSA, 2011 (in $ millions)

Leading Countries	Flow	Stock
Mauritius	45	7,330
South Africa	722	6,546
Angola	707	5,696
Nigeria	-35	4,994
Ghana	250	2,334
Equatorial Guinea	37	2,076
Liberia	113	964
Kenya	-40	292
Zambia	-1	138

Source: Analysis by CRS based on data from the Bureau of Economic Analysis (BEA).

(share of total, 2011)

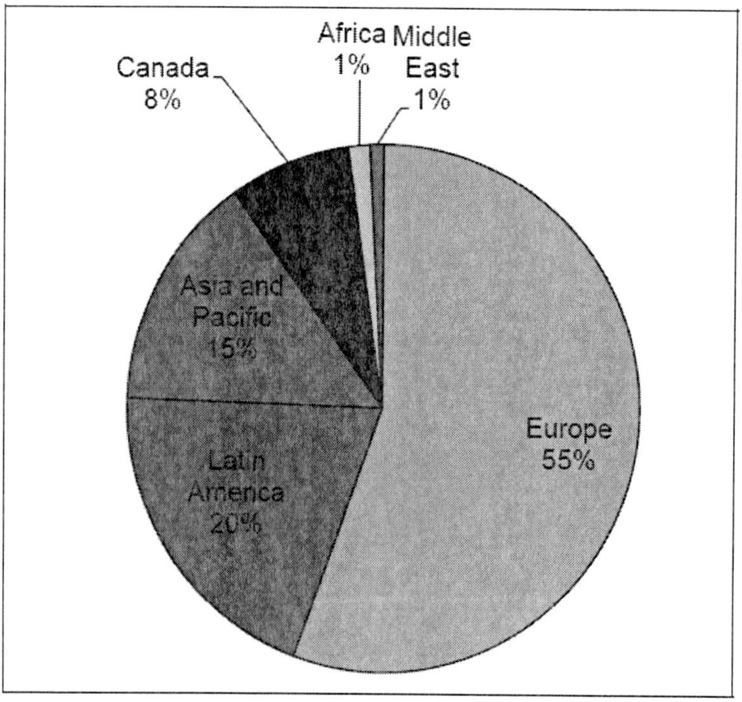

Source: Analysis by CRS based on data from the Bureau of Economic Analysis (BEA).

Figure 6. Stock of U.S. FDI Abroad, by Destination.

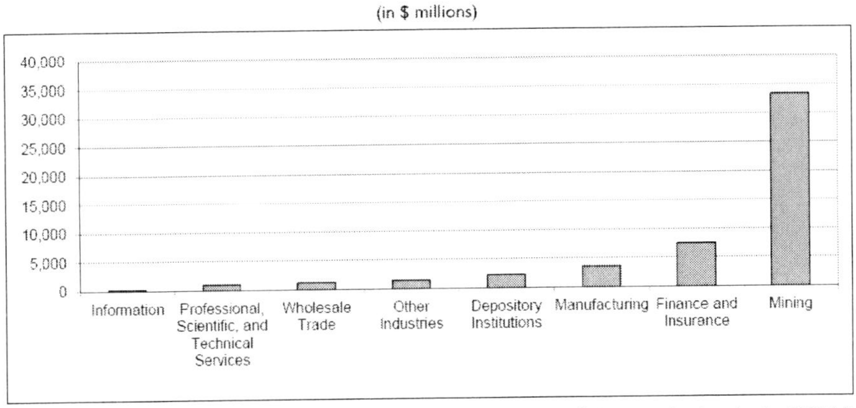

Source: Analysis by CRS based on data from the Bureau of Economic Analysis (BEA).
Note: Excludes U.S. stock of direct investment in holding companies.

Figure 7. Stock of U.S. FDI in Africa by Industry Sector, 2011.

AGOA LEGISLATION AND KEY PROVISIONS

The original AGOA legislation, the African Growth and Opportunity Act (AGOA; Title I, Trade and Development Act of 2000; P.L. 106-200), was approved by Congress in 2000, to assist the economies of sub-Saharan Africa and to improve economic relations between the United States and the region. The following section of this report examines the major provisions of AGOA, developments since enactment, and AGOA related legislation in the 112th Congress.

Beneficiary Countries

Subtitle A of AGOA authorized the President to designate sub-Saharan African countries as beneficiary countries eligible to receive duty-free treatment for certain articles that are the growth, product, or manufacture of that country. It directed that in designating a beneficiary country, the President must determine that the country (1) has established, or is making continual progress toward establishing a market-based economy and is taking other designated actions; (2) does not engage in activities that undermine U.S. national security and foreign policy interests; and (3) does not engage in gross violations of internationally recognized human rights or provide support for international terrorism.

Table 8. Beneficiary Countries under the African Growth and Opportunity Act (as of October 2012)

Republic of Angola	Republic of Ghana **	Democratic Republic of Sao Tome and Principe
Republic of Benin **	Republic of Guinea	Republic of Senegal **
Republic of Botswana **	Republic of Guinea-Bissau	Republic of Seychelles
Burkina Faso **	Republic of Kenya **	Republic of Sierra Leone **
Republic of Burundi	Kingdom of Lesotho **	Republic of South Africa
Republic of Cameroon **	Republic of Liberia **	Kingdom of Swaziland **
Republic of Cape Verde **	Republic of Malawi **	United Republic of Tanzania **
Republic of Chad **	Republic of Mali **	Republic of Togo
Union of the Comoros	Islamic Republic of Mauritania	Republic of Uganda **
Republic of Congo	Republic of Mauritius **	Republic of Zambia **
Republic of Cote d'Ivoire	Republic of Mozambique **	
Republic of Djibouti	Republic of Namibia**	
Ethiopia **	Republic of Niger **	
Gabonese Republic	Federal Republic of Nigeria **	
Republic of the Gambia **	Republic of Rwanda **	

Source: Harmonized Tariff Schedule of the United States, Supplement 1, Revision 1, October 31, 2012.

Notes: Eligible SSA countries, not currently AGOA-beneficiaries: Democratic Republic of Congo, Eritrea, Equatorial Guinea, Madagascar, Somalia, South Sudan, Sudan, and Zimbabwe.

** Beneficiary country is eligible for the lesser-developed country special rule for apparel (third-country fabric provision).

AGOA requires that the President monitor and report annually on the progress of each country in meeting the terms for AGOA eligibility. Under this requirement, Presidents have made, at the end of each year, annual designations of the countries eligible for AGOA benefits for the following year. The last presidential proclamation made with respect to AGOA was Proclamation 8741 of October 25, 2011.[35] This proclamation, among other things, reinstated the AGOA eligibility of Cote d'Ivoire, Guinea, and Niger, and also designated them each "lesser developed beneficiary sub-Saharan African countries." Thus, 40 SSA countries are now AGOA beneficiaries.

Benefits

Subtitle B of AGOA describes the trade-related benefits that are available to AGOA-eligible countries. Among these benefits is preferential duty-free treatment for certain articles under the U.S. Generalized System of Preferences (GSP). The GSP program is a unilateral trade preference regime that allows certain products from designated developing countries to enter the United States duty-free. In the AGOA Acceleration Act of 2004 (P.L. 108-274), GSP benefits were extended to AGOA countries until September 30, 2015.[36] Therefore, AGOA countries will continue to receive GSP benefits until that date, regardless of any expiration of the GSP program. AGOA beneficiaries are exempt from certain caps on allowable duty-free imports under the GSP program ("competitive need limitations").[37]

"Import-Sensitive" Articles Ineligible for GSP Preferences

1. Textile and apparel articles which were not eligible articles for purposes of this subchapter on January 1, 1994, as this subchapter was in effect on such date.
2. Watches, except those watches entered after June 30, 1989, that the President specifically determines, after public notice and comment, will not cause material injury to watch or watch band, strap, or bracelet manufacturing and assembly operations in the United States or the United States insular possessions.
3. Import-sensitive electronic articles.

4. Footwear, handbags, luggage, flat goods, work gloves, and leather wearing apparel which were not eligible articles for purposes of this subchapter on January 1, 1995, as this subchapter was in effect on such date.
5. Import-sensitive semi-manufactured and manufactured glass products.
6. Any other articles which the President determines to be import-sensitive in the context of the Generalized System of Preferences.

Source: 19 U.S.C. 2463(b).

AGOA-eligible countries may also receive duty-free treatment for certain "import sensitive" categories of products (see box above) that are identified as ineligible for duty-free treatment under GSP, provided that the President determines, after consultation with the International Trade Commission, that the product is not import-sensitive in the context of imports from AGOA beneficiaries.[38] However, the President may not grant duty-free treatment for textile or apparel products; rather, the AGOA statute provides specific benefits for certain limited categories of textiles and apparel.

Textile and Apparel Provisions

AGOA, as amended, allows duty-free and quota-free treatment for eligible textile and apparel articles in qualifying SSA countries through 2015. Qualifying articles include

- Apparel assembled in one or more AGOA beneficiary countries from U.S. yarn and fabric;
- Apparel made of SSA (regional) yarns and fabrics, subject to a cap until 2015;
- Apparel made in a designated lesser-developed country (LDC) of third-country yarns and fabrics, subject to a cap until 2015 ("Third-Country Fabric Provision Extended");
- Apparel made of yarns and fabrics not produced in commercial quantities in the United States (determination must be made that the yarn or fabric cannot be supplied by the U.S. industry in a timely manner, and to extend preferential treatment to the eligible fabric);
- Certain cashmere and merino wool sweaters;
- Eligible handloomed, handmade, or folklore articles and ethnic printed fabrics (certain countries only);

- Textiles and textile articles produced entirely in an LDC SSA beneficiary country; and
- Certain handloomed, handmade, ethnic printed fabrics, or folklore articles (certain countries only).[39]

To receive the duty-free and quota-free treatment for textile and apparel products as described above, beneficiary countries must first adopt an efficient visa ("tracking") system to prevent unlawful transshipment. They also must work with the U.S. Customs Service to report exports and prevent illegal trade. AGOA also provides that the Secretary of Commerce must monitor U.S. imports under AGOA for surges in textile and apparel imports, with the possible withdrawal of duty-free treatment if imports surge beyond a certain level.[40]

AGOA Non-Textile Rules of Origin

Non-textile products from AGOA countries must also meet certain rules of origin (ROO) requirements in order to qualify for duty-free treatment. First, duty-free entry is only allowed if the article is imported directly from the beneficiary country into the United States.

Second, at least 35% of the appraised value of the product must be the "growth, product or manufacture" of a beneficiary developing country, as defined by the sum of (1) the cost or value of materials produced in the beneficiary developing country (or any two or more beneficiary countries that are members of the same association or countries and are treated as one country for purposes of the U.S. law) plus (2) the direct costs of processing in the country.[41] Up to 15% of the required 35% of the appraised value may be of U.S. origin, and any amount of production in other beneficiary SSA countries may also contribute to the value-added requirement.[42]

Amendments to AGOA

Congress has passed legislation to amend AGOA five times since its initial passage. This legislation includes the Trade Act of 2002, the AGOA Acceleration Act of 2004, the Miscellaneous Trade and Technical Corrections Act of 2004, the Africa Investment Incentive Act of 2006, and most recently in August 2012, the amendment to AGOA that extended the third- country fabric provision ("AGOA Legislation in the 112th Congress").

Trade Act of 2002

In 2002, Congress amended AGOA for the first time through the Trade Act of 2002 (P.L. 107-210), which included adjustments to the textile and apparel provisions. An important change pertained to the cap that AGOA had set on imports of apparel assembled in an AGOA country from fabric made in an AGOA country (see the third bullet under "Textile and Apparel Provisions" above). The Trade Act of 2002 doubled this cap, increasing it to 7% in FY2008. The act, however, left the cap unchanged at 3.5% under the special rule for lesser-developed countries. The act also allowed Namibia and Botswana to qualify for the special rule for lesser-developed countries, even if their per capita incomes exceeded the limit set under AGOA. In addition, it specifically extended AGOA benefits to knit-to-shape articles and to garments cut in both the United States and an AGOA beneficiary country ("hybrid cutting") and made a correction to extend AGOA benefits to merino wool sweaters knit in AGOA beneficiary countries.

The Trade Act of 2002 also included other AGOA-related provisions. It stated that U.S. workers could be found eligible for trade adjustment assistance if U.S. production shifted to an AGOA beneficiary country and other conditions were met.[43] It authorized $9.5 million to the then-U.S. Customs Service for textile transshipment enforcement, and further specified that two permanent positions be assigned to South Africa for AGOA enforcement and that additional travel funds be allocated for verification in sub-Saharan Africa. The act also required that $1.317 million of the Customs Service budget be spent on programs to help sub-Saharan African countries develop visa and anti-transshipment systems.

AGOA Acceleration Act of 2004

In 2004, Congress further amended AGOA through the AGOA Acceleration Act of 2004 (P.L. 108-274). This legislation extended the deadline for AGOA benefits to 2015, and it also extended the special rule for LDCs from September 2004 to September 2007. It further stipulated that the cap on the volume of allowable U.S. apparel imports under this rule would be decreased starting in the year beginning September 2004, with a major reduction in the year beginning October 2006 (from 2.9% to 1.6%). The rationale behind this change was to encourage fabric production and vertical integration of the apparel industry in Africa. For apparel imports meeting the yarn forward rules of origin, the cap was set to remain at 7% until the expiration of the benefits in 2015.

The AGOA Acceleration Act also clarified certain apparel rules of origin to reflect the intent of Congress. Apparel articles containing fabric from both the United States and AGOA beneficiary countries were specifically allowed, as were otherwise eligible apparel articles containing cuffs, collars, and other similar components that did not meet the strict rules of origin. There was also clarification that ethnic printed fabric would qualify for duty-free treatment, as long as the fabric met certain standards regarding its size, form, and design characteristics. In addition, apparel articles containing fabrics and yarns recognized in the North American Free Trade Agreement (NAFTA) as being in short supply in the United States were declared as eligible for duty-free treatment, regardless of the source of such fabric and yarns. The legislation also increased the maximum allowable content of non-regional or non-U.S. fibers or yarns in AGOA eligible apparel imports, otherwise known as the *de minimis* rule, from 7% to 10%.

The AGOA Acceleration Act of 2004 also included a number of directives for the President related to trade capacity building. One such directive was to provide agricultural technical assistance by assigning U.S. personnel to at least 10 AGOA beneficiary countries, to help exporters meet U.S. technical standards for agricultural imports. Another directed the President to develop policies to encourage investment in agriculture and agricultural processing, as well as investment in infrastructure projects aimed at improving transportation and communication links both within Africa and between Africa and the United States. There was also a directive to foster improved relationships between African and U.S. customs and transportation authorities. An additional directive was to encourage technical assistance and infrastructure projects to assist in the development of the ecotourism industry in sub-Saharan Africa. Finally, another directed the President to conduct a study on each beneficiary country, identifying potential sectors for growth, barriers to such growth, and how U.S. technical assistance can assist each country in overcoming these barriers.

Miscellaneous Trade and Technical Corrections Act of 2004

In December 2004, the Miscellaneous Trade and Technical Corrections Act of 2004 (P.L. 108-429) was passed, which included a technical correction to the AGOA Acceleration Act. The legislation also allowed Mauritius to qualify for the special rule for LDCs for the one year beginning October 1, 2004, with a cap of 5% of total eligible imports under this rule.

Table 9. U.S. imports from Lesser Developed AGOA Countries under the Third- Country Fabric Provision (in millions of square meter equivalents (M2))

	2010	2011	YTD September 2011	YTD September 2012
Total Quota Allowance	814.400	866.700	866.700	938.700
Total Imports	191.648	199.857	153.464	143.131
Kenya	68.097	74.476	58.321	53.513
Lesotho	71.702	64.630	48.635	50.838
Swaziland	26.800	19.991	16.957	10.948
Mauritius	11.731	17.930	13.447	12.858
Tanzania	3.332	6.942	5.216	7.02
Ethiopia	2.949	6.128	4.292	3.313
Malawi	4.066	4.689	3.097	1.445
Botswana	2.431	3.292	2.433	2.771
Ghana	0.188	1.610	1.61	0.913
Uganda	0.087	0.138	0.138	0.000
Cameroon	0.001	0.016	0.001	0.000
Mozambique	0.000	0.014	0.014	0.000
Liberia	0.000	0.000	0.000	0.000

Source: Office of Textiles and Apparel, Department of Commerce.

Africa Investment Incentive Act of 2006

Congress passed the Africa Investment Incentive Act of 2006 in December 2006 (Title VI of P.L. 109-432), which extended the textile and apparel benefits of AGOA until 2015. This act also extended until 2012 the special rule for LDCs, which allows textiles and apparel quota- and duty-free access to the U.S. market regardless of the source of materials used, as long as assembly takes place within an AGOA-eligible LDC. The act also increases the cap on square meter equivalents under this rule back to the initial level of 3.5%. It also contains an "abundant supply" provision stipulating that if a certain fabric is determined by the U.S. International Trade Commission to be available in commercial quantities in AGOA beneficiary countries, then the special rule will no longer apply to apparel and textiles containing that particular fabric.

Table 10. Top Ten Apparel Exporters under AGOA (actual $ U.S.)

Country	2011 (Value)
Lesotho	314,311,152
Kenya	258,886,230
Mauritius	153,428,075
Swaziland	76,579,510
Botswana	15,475,230
Malawi	13,483,949
Ethiopia	9,966,621
South Africa	5,277,269
Tanzania	5,118,819
Ghana	1,267,006
Total Above	853,793,861
All Other	1,021,392
Total	854,815,253

Source: U.S. International Trade Commission Trade Dataweb, http://www.usitc.gov.
Note: Imports for Consumption.

AGOA Legislation in the 112th Congress

Third-Country Fabric Provision Extended

A provision in AGOA that allows duty-free treatment of apparel assembled in one or more lesser- developed SSA countries regardless of the country of origin of the fabric ("third-country fabric provision"), subject to a cap, was recently extended by Congress through September 2015 (P.L. 112-163). This amendment also added South Sudan to the list of SSA countries eligible for AGOA benefits, though full beneficiary status also requires approval by the Administration.

Lesser-developed countries are defined in AGOA as those with a per capita gross national product of less than $1,500 per year as measured by the World Bank.[44] In subsequent amendments to AGOA, Botswana, Namibia, and Mauritius were added to the list of lesser-developed countries (§112 of P.L. 106-200, as amended). At present, 27 AGOA-eligible countries qualify for the third- country fabric provision (see **Table 8**).

The quantitative limitation on third-country fabric, set each fiscal year, is announced annually by the Committee for the Implementation of Textile Agreements (CITA).[45] The AGOA Acceleration Act of 2004 raised the quantitative limit to a maximum of 3.5% (by quantity) of all U.S. apparel imports. In October 2012, CITA announced that the amount imported under this provision, for the 12-month period beginning October 1, 2012, must be no more than 867,929,963 square meters equivalent (SMEs), half of all apparel imports allowed under AGOA provisions.[46] Any imports from qualifying SSA countries in excess of these quantities are subject to otherwise applicable tariffs.[47] As **Table 9** indicates, imports under the provision from eligible countries are far below the quota allowance.[48]

The fact that only 23% of the allowable third-country fabric provision quota is currently being used could mask the fact that several SSA countries, including Lesotho, Kenya, Mauritius, Swaziland, and Botswana, have exported a significant amount (both by quantity and value) of apparel under the provision (see **Table 10**). For the countries above—all of whom, with the exception of Botswana, are major beneficiaries of AGOA by percentage of utilization (see **Table 11**)—U.S. apparel imports represent the major portion of their benefits under the AGOA preference.

Pending Legislation

H.R. 656 (introduced February 11, 2011), in part, directs the President to establish a Special Representative for United States-Africa Trade, Development, and Diaspora Affairs within the U.S. Department of State. The role of the representative would be to promote U.S.-African trade and investment relations; facilitate international learning exchanges; establish a database for information sharing; and consult with African governments, the private sector, and United Nations agencies regarding economic development in Africa. This bill is currently in committee.

H.R. 4221 (introduced March 20, 2012) and its companion bill in the Senate, S. 2215 (introduced March 21, 2012), seek to increase U.S. exports to Africa, in part, through strategies aimed at further developing relationships between the United States and African countries on a government-to-government level, as well as fostering private sector U.S.-African ties and targeting more U.S. export financing toward U.S.-SSA trade. Hearings were held on this legislation in the House Committee on Foreign Affairs Subcommittee on Africa, Global Health, and Human Rights on April 17, 2012, and in the Senate Committee on Foreign Relations Subcommittee on African Affairs on July 25, 2012. The Senate Committee on Foreign Relations voted to report out an amended version of S. 2215 on September 19, 2012. The House version of the bill is still in committee.

Table 11. Total U.S. Imports, Imports under AGOA (including GSP), and Utilization Rate of Preference, 2011 (actual $ U.S.)

AGOA Beneficiary (in 2011)	Total U.S. Imports	Imports Under AGOA (including GSP)	Utilization Rate of Preference (%)
Chad	3,188,885,282	2,991,225,667	93.80%
Swaziland	83,289,612	77,192,451	92.68%
Nigeria	33,834,587,752	31,008,519,187	91.65%
Angola	13,756,357,845	11,534,181,604	83.85%
Malawi	72,353,659	60,141,734	83.12%
Lesotho	384,351,085	314,335,330	81.78%
Congo (ROC)	2,376,790,086	1,935,228,815	81.42%
Kenya	380,463,239	292,594,742	76.90%
Mauritius	250,482,636	169,190,565	67.55%
Ghana	778,992,716	454,534,351	58.35%
Cameroon	322,218,673	173,784,645	53.93%
South Africa	9,473,431,885	3,797,405,595	40.08%
Namibia	436,337,789	134,316,828	30.78%
Cape Verde	1,467,584	165,226	11.26%
Gabon	4,432,128,840	477,555,593	10.77%
Tanzania	58,244,222	5,751,382	9.87%
Ethiopia	144,404,059	13,874,923	9.61%
Senegal	6,766,267	490,660	7.25%
Gambia	82,442	5,352	6.49%
Botswana	293,285,806	17,063,293	5.82%
Uganda	45,881,727	2,540,952	5.54%
Mali	4,078,609	132,542	3.25%
Sao Tome & Principe	981,624	24,482	2.49%
Mozambique	34,966,794	692,543	1.98%
Rwanda	30,857,888	597,270	1.94%
Djibouti	4,053,092	58,050	1.43%
Sierra Leone	26,480,435	193,761	0.73%
Benin	1,970,887	14,019	0.71%
Zambia	47,321,448	220,669	0.47%
Burkina Faso	3,603,288	6,623	0.18%
Togo	31,744,687	57,584	0.18%
Liberia	158,178,415	0	0.00%
Burundi	9,558,071	0	0.00%
Seychelles	6,265,409	0	0.00%
Comoros	1,778,891	0	0.00%
Mauritania	965,142	0	0.00%
Guinea-Bissau	261,369	0	0.00%

Source: U.S. International Trade Commission Trade Dataweb (http://dataweb.usitc.gov).

Note: "Utilization Rate of Preference" is the value of U.S. imports under AGOA divided by the total amount of U.S. imports from AGOA countries expressed as a percentage. U.S. Imports for Consumption

AGOA Trade Trends

According to the United States Trade Representative (USTR), over 93% of U.S. imports from SSA from AGOA-eligible countries in 2010 entered the United States duty-free, either under AGOA or GSP, or under zero-duty most-favored-nation (MFN) tariff rates.49 In 2011, U.S. imports under AGOA and GSP amounted to $53.8 billion (see **Table 11**).

Table 12. Top Ten U.S. Imports under AGOA (Excluding GSP) (actual $ U.S.)

HTS Number	2010	2011	Percent Change
27-Mineral fuels and oil	35,833,825,932	48,497,450,862	35.30%
87- Vehicles, Except Railway Or Tramway, And Parts	1,538,204,237	2,038,110,536	32.50%
62-Articles of apparel and clothing accessories, not knitted or crocheted	368,059,665	445,373,100	21.00%
61-Articles of apparel and clothing accessories, knitted or crocheted	358,416,707	409,442,153	14.20%
72-Iron and steel	141,893,313	204,501,643	44.10%
08-Edible fruit and nuts; peel of citrus fruit or melons	104,371,648	100,871,339	-3.40%
38-Miscellaneous chemical products	41,692,091	47,955,570	15.00%
22-Beverages, spirits, and vinegar	52,759,899	47,657,887	-9.70%
24-Tobacco and manufactured tobacco substitutes	33,362,905	39,949,659	19.70%
20-Preparations of vegetables, fruit, nuts, or other parts of plants	18,275,960	17,720,158	-3.00%
Subtotal	38,490,862,357	51,849,032,907	34.70%
All Other	26,903,235	34,021,330	26.50%
Total	38,517,765,592	51,883,054,237	34.70%

Source: U.S. International Trade Commission Trade Dataweb, http://www.usitc.gov.
Notes: Imports under AGOA are a subset of imports from SSA.

In 2011, oil and mineral fuels (mostly crude oil) accounted for about 93% of all U.S. imports (by value) under the African Growth and Opportunity Act (AGOA), and about 81% of all U.S. imports from all SSA countries.50 Vehicles and parts were the next-largest category of AGOA imports at 4%. Apparel products (HTS chapters 61 and 62 combined) amounted to about 2%.[51]

As shown in **Figure 8**, the largest portion, by far, of U.S. exports to SSA are to AGOA-eligible countries. Except for decreases in 2002 and 2009-2010, arguably due to periods of worldwide recession, these exports have increased markedly over time. As **Table 13** indicates, the top destinations for U.S. products are South Africa, Nigeria, Angola, and Ghana.

AGOA Technical Assistance and Capacity Building

Section 122 of AGOA directed the President to target U.S. government technical assistance and trade capacity building in AGOA beneficiary countries. This mandate includes assistance to both government and non-governmental actors.

The act directs the President to target technical assistance to governments to (1) liberalize trade and exports; (2) harmonize laws and regulations with WTO membership; (3) engage in financial and fiscal restructuring; and (4) promote greater agribusiness linkages. The act also includes assistance for developing private sector business associations and networks among U.S. and sub-Saharan African enterprises. Technical assistance is also to be targeted to increasing the number of reverse trade missions, increasing trade in services, addressing critical agricultural policy issues, and building capabilities of African states to participate in the World Trade Organization, generally, and particularly in services. In FY2010 (latest available data), the United States reported obligating approximately $588 million in trade capacity building (TCB) assistance to AGOA countries.[52] Of this amount, about $341 million was obligated for physical infrastructure development and $200 million on trade-related agriculture projects.[53]

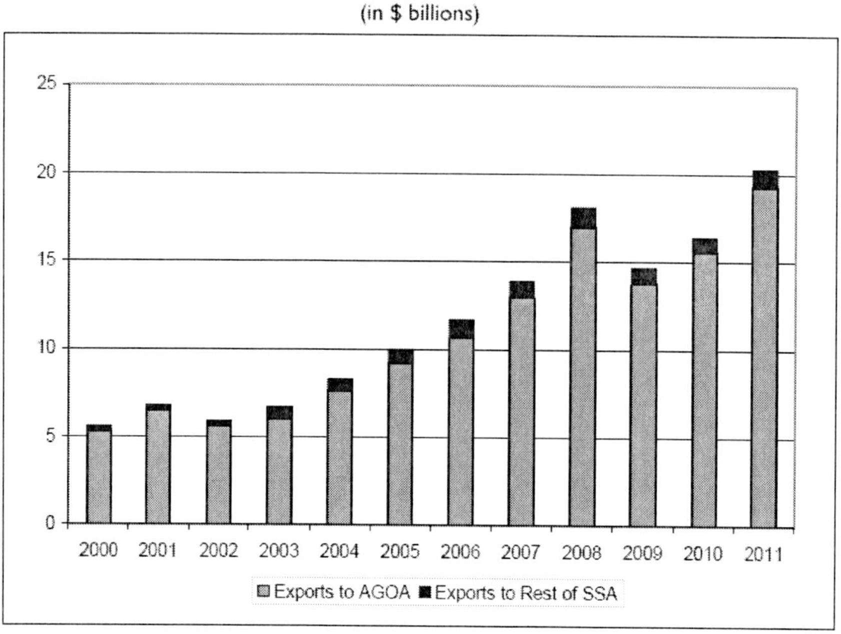

Source: U.S. International Trade Commission Trade Dataweb, http://dataweb.usitc.gov.

Note: U.S. Domestic Exports, FAS Value.

Figure 8. U.S. Exports to AGOA-Eligible Countries as a Portion of Total U.S. Exports to sub-Saharan Africa.

United States–sub-Saharan Africa Trade and Economic Cooperation Forum

Under AGOA, the President was required to establish within a year of enactment, after consultation with Congress and the other governments concerned, a United States-sub-Saharan Africa Trade and Economic Cooperation Forum (hereinafter referred to as the Forum). The act stated that the President was to direct certain top officials to host the first Forum meeting with their counterparts from AGOA-eligible countries and countries attempting to meet AGOA eligibility requirements.[54] The purpose of the Forum is to "discuss expanding trade and investment relations between the United States and sub-Saharan Africa and the implementation of [AGOA] including encouraging joint ventures between small and large businesses."

AGOA also required the President to encourage non-governmental organizations and the private sector to hold similar annual meetings, and it required the President to instruct U.S. delegates to the Forum to promote a review of HIV/AIDS in each sub-Saharan African country and the effect on economic development. It required the President to meet, to the extent practicable, with heads of governments of sub-Saharan African countries at least every two years to discuss expanding trade and investment relations, and the first such meeting should be within one year of enactment.

Table 13. U.S. Exports to AGOA Countries, 2011 (actual $ U.S.)

Country	2011
South Africa	6,848,590,454
Nigeria	4,706,183,368
Angola	1,458,062,000
Ghana	1,155,466,454
Ethiopia	684,957,626
Benin	610,363,392
Kenya	447,392,579
Mozambique	445,907,638
Senegal	258,781,861
Tanzania	250,729,324
Mauritania	241,472,844
Country	2011
Congo (ROC)	222,429,871
Cameroon	216,235,118
Togo	212,522,913
Gabon	197,360,657
Liberia	184,975,506
Djibouti	130,577,790
Zambia	123,078,281
Namibia	121,006,058
Rwanda	118,576,796
Subtotal Above Countries	18,634,670,530
All Other	590,328,884
Total Exports	19,224,999,414

Source: U.S. International Trade Commission Trade Dataweb (http://dataweb.usitc.gov).

Notes: Total Exports, FAS value.

AGOA was enacted May 18, 2000, and on May 16, 2001, President Bush established the Forum and announced plans for its first meeting in Washington in October 2001. The first Forum was held October 29-30, 2001, in Washington, DC. President Bush addressed the Forum and announced several initiatives: (1) a $200 million Overseas Private Investment Corporation (OPIC) support facility to give U.S. firms access to loans, guarantees, and political risk insurance for investment projects; (2) a regional office of the Trade and Development Agency (TDA) in Johannesburg to help attract new investment; and (3) the Trade for African Development and Enterprise Program, initially funded at $15 million, to establish regional hubs to help African businesses in the global market. (These initiatives were implemented; see discussion below.)

AGOA forums have been held annually since 2001, alternately in the United States or in an SSA partner country. The 10th AGOA forum was held in Zambia on June 9-10, 2011. The theme of the Forum was "Enhanced Trade Through Increased Competitiveness, Value Addition, and Deeper Regional Integration."

The 11th AGOA Forum was held in Washington, DC, June 14-15, 2012. The theme for this year's event was "Enhancing Africa's Infrastructure for Trade," and it focused on various aspects designed to promote trade, including improvements in both physical infrastructure, such as roads and ports, and institutional infrastructure, such as the business climate. The Forum also focused on advancing African initiatives in regional economic integration and increasing awareness among U.S. businesses of opportunities in Africa. In a speech at the Forum, Secretary of State Hillary Rodham Clinton called for "urgent" efforts to renew the AGOA third country fabric provision. Continuing with the Forum's focus on improved infrastructure, she also highlighted the need for more "human infrastructure," or investments in human capital, especially among young people, throughout the region.

The Forum was followed by a one-time event, the *U.S.-Africa Business Conference 2012*, held in Cincinnati, OH, June 21-22. Hosted by the State Department and several other U.S. government agencies and private business promotion groups,[55] the conference sought

> to expand on the AGOA Forum by providing an opportunity to both showcase U.S. business expertise to potential African clients, and to highlight trade and investment opportunities in Africa to U.S. exporters and investors … [focused] broadly on infrastructure development, including energy, transportation, and water and sanitation.[56]

U.S. Agency for International Development (USAID)

AGOA's mandate to encourage trade-related technical assistance is primarily implemented by USAID through the African Global Competitiveness Initiative (AGCI), a Presidential Initiative which supplanted the Trade for African Development and Enterprise (TRADE) initiative in 2006. The TRADE initiative succeeded the Africa Trade and Investment Policy Program (ATRIP), which operated from 1998 to 2003. These initiatives are generally used to focus activities around a common goal, but there are AGOA-related activities funded by other initiatives within USAID.

USAID funds various technical assistance programs throughout Africa aimed at improving trade within the region and between the region and the United States. USAID supports regional efforts through its regional missions and the four Regional Hubs for Global Competitiveness (Trade Hubs), located in Ghana, Senegal, Kenya, and Botswana. USAID bilateral missions support projects in individual African countries. The missions and hubs work on improving trade policy both regionally and within country governments. They also have programs to improve trade infrastructure, such as in transportation and energy, and they have enterprise development programs which often target specific industries, such as handicrafts and shea butter.

As mentioned above, AGOA encourages the establishment of private sector linkages between U.S. and SSA businesses. To this end, USAID funds an international business linkage program, South African International Business Linkages (SAIBL), which is implemented by the Corporate Council on Africa. SAIBL assists black-owned South African companies to prepare business plans, achieve International Standards Organization (ISO) certification, participate in U.S.-led trade delegations, attend trade shows in the United States, and identify public and private sector export financing. It also assists U.S. firms by identifying trade and investment opportunities in South Africa, by steering U.S. firms to appropriate government and private sector contacts, and by identifying sources of financing. USAID formerly funded a similar linkage program for West Africa, the West African International Business Linkages (WAIBL), but it no longer funds this program. The regional trade hubs implement many of the same types of activities as SAIBL, except that they focus more on promoting trade in general and not just exports to the United States.

Assistant U.S. Trade Representative for Africa (AUSTRA)

Section 117 of AGOA supported the creation of this position to serve as the "primary point of contact in the executive branch for those persons engaged in trade between the United States and sub-Saharan Africa," and the chief adviser to the U.S. Trade Representative (USTR) on trade and investment issues pertaining to Africa. This position previously had been established by President Clinton in 1998. One primary function of AUSTRA is to make the yearly determinations as to which countries are eligible for AGOA benefits generally, and also its special textile and apparel benefits. The AUSTRA also sponsors projects for WTO training for SSA trade negotiators and provides support for the Trade Advisory Committee on Africa.

Overseas Private Investment Corporation (OPIC)

Section 123 of AGOA expressed the sense of Congress that OPIC should exercise its authority to support projects in SSA and directed OPIC to increase funds directed to SSA countries. OPIC, a U.S. development finance agency, seeks to promote economic growth in developing and emerging economies and expand U.S. exports by providing political risk insurance, project financing, investment funds support, and other services for U.S. businesses in those countries, in support of U.S. foreign policy goals. OPIC's programs are intended to promote U.S. private investment by mitigating risks, such as political risks (including currency inconvertibility, expropriation, political violence, and terrorism), for U.S. firms making qualified investment overseas. Since 1974, OPIC has supported investments of nearly $6.3 billion in projects in Africa (of about $200 billion worldwide).[57]

Export-Import Bank (Ex-Im Bank)

Ex-Im Bank is the official export credit agency of the U.S. government. It maintains finance and insurance programs to facilitate U.S. exports to developing countries, especially in circumstances in which alternative commercial financing is not available, in order to contribute to U.S. employment. Some Ex-Im Bank programs are used to counter officially backed subsidized export financing offered by other countries. Its main program instruments are direct loans, loan guarantees, working capital guarantees, and export credit insurance, all backed by the full faith and credit of the U.S. government.[58]

Section 124 of AGOA expressed the sense of Congress that the Ex-Im Bank should continue to expand its financial commitments to its loan guarantee and insurance programs to African countries. The legislation also commended the Bank's sub-Saharan Africa Advisory Committee for its work in fostering economic cooperation between the United States and SSA. This committee's work was extended to September 30, 2014, in recent legislation reauthorizing the Ex-Im Bank (§23 of P.L. 112-122).[59]

In FY2011, the Ex-Im Bank authorized nearly $1.4 billion to support U.S. exports to SSA countries ($804 million in direct loans, $466 million in loan guarantees, $68 million in export credit insurance, and $40 million working capital guarantees), which supported approximately 8% of U.S. exports to SSA.[60] Ex-Im Bank-supported exports to SSA have tripled since 2007 from $434 million to about $1.4 billion in FY2011. About 80% of the number of those transactions directly supported small businesses.[61]

U.S. and Foreign Commercial Service (CS)

The U.S. and Foreign Commercial Service is the main export promotion arm of the U.S. Department of Commerce's International Trade Administration. CS services are primarily targeted at small and medium-sized U.S. businesses, providing export promotion services such as trade counseling, market intelligence, business matchmaking, and commercial diplomacy tools to assist them in exporting abroad. In 2011, CS employed about 500 staff working in the United States, operating 108 "U.S. Export Assistance Centers." CS also staffs 115 offices in more than 70 countries (down from 125 offices in 75 countries in 2010), which employ about 900 overseas staff, including Foreign Service officers and locally employed staff.[62] In 45 other countries where the CS does not have a presence, it has an agreement with the State Department to fulfill these functions through its Foreign Service officers and locally employed staff.[63]

In Section 125 of AGOA, Congress found that the CS presence in SSA had been reduced since the 1980s and that the level of staffing in 1997 (seven officers in four countries) did not "adequately service the needs of U.S. businesses attempting to do business in sub-Saharan Africa."[64] Accordingly, the legislation required the posting of at least 20 CS officers in not less than 10 countries in SSA by December 31, 2001, "subject to the availability of appropriations."[65] According to the U.S. Commercial Service Annual Report for 2011, there are currently eight CS staff in Africa. CS staff are located in Accra, Ghana; Nairobi, Kenya; and Cape Town and Johannesburg, South Africa.[66]

Section 125(c) of P.L. 106-200 (AGOA) also directed the International Trade Administration (ITA) to develop an initiative to (1) identify the best U.S. export prospects in the region; (2) identify tariff and non-tariff barriers that impede U.S. exports to Africa; and (3) undertake discussions with African states to increase market access for these goods and services. These activities are being carried out, in part, by the ITA's Market Access and Compliance Unit (MAC). The ITA also maintains the AGOA website at http://www.agoa.gov.

U.S. Trade and Development Agency (TDA)

Though its role is not specifically mentioned in AGOA legislation, the TDA is an independent agency that operates under a dual mission of promoting economic development and U.S. commercial interests in developing and middle-income countries. The agency links U.S. businesses to export opportunities by funding project planning activities, feasibility studies, and pilot projects overseas; and by sponsoring reverse trade missions, while creating sustainable infrastructure and economic growth in partner countries. TDA supports projects in economic sectors such as transportation, energy, and telecommunications. It provides grants to overseas project sponsors (both public and private sector grantees) who select U.S. companies to conduct TDA-funded activities. These programs are designed to assist project sponsors to make informed investment decisions, while opening markets for increased exports of U.S.-manufactured goods and services. Since 1981, TDA has provided over $90 million for projects in SSA, which the agency states have resulted in over $1 billion in U.S. exports related to partnerships between African project sponsors and U.S. firms. In FY2010, TDA obligated funds for 39 projects in SSA totaling $9.3 million, or approximately 19% of its total program expenditures ($49.7 million).[67]

Multilateral Initiatives

In addition to domestic agency programs, the United States participates in several multilateral institutions that provide trade capacity building in Africa and other developing-country regions and indirectly support the aims of AGOA. The World Bank and regional development banks all provide trade capacity building assistance, mainly in the form of loans.

The Enhanced Integrated Framework (EIF) is the main multilateral initiative in trade capacity building. It is a process that assists least developed countries (LDCs) to integrate trade issues into their national development strategies. The EIF process begins with a diagnostic study of trade challenges and opportunities in the LDC, and is meant to result in better targeted and coordinated assistance by all donors. Six international institutions collaborate on the EIF, including the International Monetary Fund (IMF), the International Trade Center (ITC), the United Nations Conference on Trade and Development (UNCTAD), the United Nations Development Program (UNDP), the World Bank, and the WTO. The EIF is funded by an Multi-Donor Trust Fund, composed of voluntary contributions from multilateral and bilateral donors. Total contribution receipts to this trust fund equaled $165.1 million as of April 2012, of which the United States contributed $600,000.[68]

The United States has also provided SSA countries with technical assistance and TCB support on a wide range of WTO-related issues such as trade facilitation, services, and sanitary and phytosanitary measures, in coordination with the other multilateral institutions mentioned above.[69] The United States has also provided technical support for the efforts of some SSA countries, such as Ethiopia (still in negotiations) and Togo (WTO accession July 2007), to accede to the WTO.[70]

Regional Cooperation and Free Trade Agreements

P.L. 105-200, the original AGOA legislation, contained a section encouraging exploration of new agreements to encourage trade and investment. AGOA, however, directed the President specifically toward FTA negotiations, and required more concrete steps regarding potential actions to be taken to establish such an agreement.

Discussion of potential partners for free trade agreements has revolved around South Africa and the South African Customs Union (SACU), but several other regional groupings are potential partners for future trade agreements with the United States. The Southern African Development Community (SADC), the Common Market for Eastern and Southern Africa (COMESA), the East African Community (EAC), and the West African Economic and Monetary Union (WAEMU) have all taken steps to begin the process of economic integration, either through trade liberalization or through steps to promote monetary union. While these groups are being encouraged in their attempts at regional integration, they are not immediate prospects for FTAs with the United States. Background on these groups appears in **Appendix A**.

FTA Negotiations with SACU

On November 4, 2002, then-USTR Robert B. Zoellick notified Congress that negotiations would be initiated with the SACU member countries.[71] These negotiations began in June 2003, but were postponed indefinitely in April 2006. Observers cited several possible reasons for the unsuccessful FTA negotiations, including the capacity of SACU nations to negotiate a U.S.-style (comprehensive and high-standard) FTA, and disagreements between the parties on the scope and level of ambition of the negotiations.

The United States and SACU signed a Trade, Investment, and Development Cooperation Agreement (TIDCA) on July 16, 2008, designed to build on and potentially capture some of the progress made in previous FTA negotiations.[72] The TIDCA establishes a forum for consultative discussions and cooperative work, and creates a framework for discussions on customs and trade facilitation, technical barriers to trade, sanitary and phytosanitary measures, and trade and investment relations.[73]

The U.S. decision to negotiate an FTA with SACU, rather than just with South Africa, may have reflected the large degree of economic integration that exists among the SACU states. The original SACU agreement dates from the colonial government in 1910 and was renegotiated with the apartheid government in 1969. A new agreement to more fully integrate the smaller states into decision-making for the area, which was previously dominated by South Africa, was signed on October 21, 2002. The agreement is characterized by free movement of goods within SACU, a common external tariff, and the common revenue pool which is apportioned among the member states.

However, South Africa remains the dominant economy of the region, accounting for 87% of the population and 91% of the gross domestic product of the customs area (2010 figures).[74]

U.S. merchandise exports to SACU totaled $7.0 billion in 2011, led by machinery, motor vehicles and parts, precious metals and stones, mineral fuels and oils, precision equipment (e.g., photographic and optical devices), electrical machinery and parts, and aircraft. U.S. merchandise imports from SACU in 2011 totaled $10.7 billion, and included precious metals and stones, motor vehicles and parts, iron and steel, and machinery.[75]

U.S. Trade and Investment Framework Agreements (TIFAs)

Although TIFAs were not specifically addressed in AGOA legislation, the USTR regards TIFAs as important tools for strengthening trade and economic relations with key SSA countries and regional organizations.[76] As of this writing, the United States has negotiated TIFAs with Angola, Ghana, Liberia, Mauritius, Mozambique, Nigeria, Rwanda, and South Africa, and with the COMESA,[77] East African Community, and the WAEMU[78] regional arrangements. Generally, TIFAs commit the signatories to expand trade of goods and services, to encourage private sector investment, and to resolve problems and disputes through consultation and dialogue. To facilitate these objectives, the signatories of each agreement have established a Council on Trade and Investment to provide a venue for consultation on trade issues of interest or concern to the parties, and to work toward the removal of impediments to trade and investment flows. TIFAs are often considered to be first steps to the negotiation of free trade agreements.

U.S. Bilateral Investment Treaties (BIT)

BITs were not specifically addressed in AGOA, but are regarded as important tools for advancing bilateral trade. BITs help protect U.S. foreign direct investment and promote economic growth by advancing important reforms and encouraging the adoption of policies that facilitate and support foreign investment.[79] As of this writing, the United States has signed BITs with Cameroon, Republic of the Congo (Brazzaville), Democratic Republic of the Congo (Kinshasa), Mozambique, Rwanda, and Senegal, and is currently pursuing a BIT with the East African Community (EAC). The goals of the BIT are to protect U.S. investments abroad, and to encourage market-oriented domestic policy in host countries. Generally, BITs ensure national treatment for U.S. investments, limit expropriations, enable free repatriation of funds, place limitations on the imposition of trade-distorting or inefficient practices on U.S. investments—including requirements in hiring—and provide the right of submission of investment disputes to international arbitration. These treaties are promoted by the U.S. government as a method of encouraging the development of international law and trade standards within the partner country.[80]

AGOA: Current and Future Challenges

Several issues may be important to Congress in the oversight of AGOA and in consideration of a potential renewal of the preference program. These issues concern the diversification of beneficiary country and industry participants, the continued eligibility of certain countries for AGOA benefits, the HIV/AIDS epidemic, and the participation of U.S. small business in AGOA.

- **Diversification of AGOA Exports.** While textile and manufacturing industries make up a growing part of U.S. imports under AGOA, these imports are dwarfed by AGOA imports from the petroleum and mining sectors. These industries are highly capitalized and do not provide extensive employment opportunities for African workers. AGOA benefits are also concentrated in few countries. Moreover, several AGOA-eligible countries export very little under the program. Increasing African economic diversification and export levels, key goals of AGOA, could arguably be enhanced by continuing and potentially expanding targeted trade capacity building and technical assistance to countries in the sub- region, particularly in the sectors where economic activity and production is concentrated. Agriculture, for instance, is a crucial component of many African economies and an important source of income for African workers. Increasing agricultural exports under AGOA, notably of processed goods, could help raise incomes and spur economic growth. Similarly, targeted technical assistance aimed at improving productive capacity, infrastructure, and investment policies, could also spur growth in light manufactured product exports.

AGOA IN COMPARATIVE PERSPECTIVE: EUROPEAN UNION TRADE FRAMEWORKS WITH AFRICA

Like the United States, the European Union (EU) has also been active in promoting trade between itself and SSA countries. The EU-South Africa Agreement on Trade, Development, and Cooperation entered into force on January 1, 2000. This agreement creates a free-trade area between the participants during a 12-year asymmetric transition period. The EU pledged to remove tariffs on 95% of imports from South Africa during a 10-year period with most products granted duty-free status in 2002. South Africa will remove duties on 86% of its tariff lines during a 12-year period with most eliminations occurring between 2006 and 2012. Notably, the agreement does not provide tariff relief to several important South African agricultural exports, nor to aluminum.

The Cotonou Agreement, signed in Cotonou, Benin, between the European Union and 71 African, Caribbean, and Pacific nations (ACP) in February 2000, extended non-reciprocal, duty-free access for industrial and processed agricultural goods to the EU market granted by the 4th Lomé Convention to the end of 2007. The extent of the duty- free access conferred by Cotonou was subsequently enhanced in March 2001 by the "Everything but Arms" initiative, which granted LDCs tariff-free access to all goods, except for sugar, rice, and bananas, for which products a tariff-rate quota system was maintained during a phase-out period ending in 2009. Provisions of the Cotonou Agreement call for the negotiation of trade liberalization agreements with regional economic partnerships that could include the regional African groupings discussed in **Appendix A**.
Preliminary negotiations on the Regional Economic Partnership Agreements (EPAs) began on September 27, 2002, and were supposed to conclude before the expiration of the Cotonou Agreement on December 31, 2007. Many African countries opposed signing EPAs because that would mean opening up their markets to EU imports. In the end, a temporary compromise was reached: most African countries signed "interim EPAs" to keep their EU trade preferences as they were under the Cotonou Agreement.

On May 14, 2012, the first EPA between the EU and Mauritius, Madagascar, Seychelles, and Zimbabwe went into effect. These countries will have duty-free/quota-free access to the EU market for exports.

In exchange, these countries agreed to open their markets to EU exports in a 15-year time frame, but may exclude products they consider import sensitive.[81]

- **Eligibility Standards.** A country's eligibility for AGOA benefits may become a subject of controversy. Some observers feel that the President must strictly enforce eligibility requirements to ensure continued adherence to reforms. However, others have cited the unpredictability of a country's AGOA benefits from year-to-year as a source of investment risk, and have suggested minimum eligibility terms of greater than the current one-year period. Another suggestion includes allowing Congress to override the President's decision to terminate AGOA benefits through legislation. Several countries have been considered candidates for losing AGOA eligibility.[82]
- **HIV/AIDS.** The HIV/AIDS pandemic continues to destabilize the economies of Africa and threatens any progress achieved by AGOA as additional income is spent, not to raising living standards, but to treat a population afflicted with the disease. Due to the disease, life expectancy is falling in several AGOA-eligible countries and in the region as a whole. Even with the advantages that AGOA preferences confer, investors may be deterred from the region by high medical costs, by constant replacement of workers stricken with the disease and the attendant training costs, and by the destabilizing risks associated with a society containing a large, dying population.
- **Lack of Uniform Trade Effects Reporting.** The initial AGOA legislation required an annual comprehensive report on U.S.-Africa trade and investment policy and on implementation of AGOA. The resulting annual report was a unique and invaluable oversight and trade trend tracking tool for policy-makers, but the reporting requirement sunsetted in 2008. Congress may wish to consider reinstating the annual AGOA reporting requirement.
- **Small Business Participation.** Small business accounts for about 55% of the U.S. GDP, and employs a large portion of American workers. U.S. small businesses, however, only participate in limited trade with Africa, and reportedly very few in the small business community know about AGOA. Some observers have noted that U.S. small businesses may benefit from AGOA, and in the process help provide avenues for diversifying African exports. Small business is also important in Africa, and increased partnership may result in

better participation on both continents. There are multiple ways that U.S. agencies could become more involved in increasing awareness of AGOA among the small business community, and providing opportunities for partnership. Examples include increased investment in and emphasis on the use of USAID's trade hubs as a mechanism for U.S. small business entrance into Africa, or an increased small business emphasis within the mandate of the U.S. Foreign Commercial Service. The provision of appropriations adequate to enable greater CS compliance with the original AGOA goal of deploying at least 20 CS officers in not less than 10 African countries could also further attainment of the goals laid out under AGOA.

Appendix A. Regional Economic Integration Among sub-Saharan Africa Nations

Southern African Development Community (SADC)

This group is composed of the nations of Angola, Botswana, Democratic Republic of the Congo, Lesotho, Madagascar, Malawi, Mauritius, Mozambique, Namibia, South Africa, Swaziland, Tanzania, Zambia, and Zimbabwe. Originally formed by front-line states to lessen economic dependence on the apartheid regime in South Africa, the group expanded to include South Africa in 1994. The 1996 Protocol on Trade committed each signatory to remove duties and non-tariff barriers to SADC members within 12 years, to provide national treatment for each other's goods, and to bind existing tariffs at current levels.

Common Market for Eastern and Southern Africa (COMESA)

Founded in 1982 as the Preferential Trade Area of Eastern and Southern Africa, current member states of the COMESA include Burundi, Comoros, Democratic Republic of the Congo, Eritrea, Ethiopia, Kenya, Madagascar, Malawi, Mauritius, Rwanda, Seychelles, Sudan, Swaziland, Uganda, Zambia, and Zimbabwe. The goal of COMESA is to attain a "fully integrated, competitive, regional economic community with high standards of living for all its people ready to merge into an African Economic Community."[83] The goal of monetary union by 2025 is expected to be advanced by the introduction of limited currency convertibility and improved coordination of fiscal and monetary policy during this time period.

East African Community (EAC)

Comprised of Burundi, Kenya, Rwanda, Tanzania, and Uganda, this organization sought to revive historic regional integration arrangements that had existed since 1917. This cooperation broke down in the 1970s due to widespread transshipments and the varied economic paths of its participants. The community was established once again by the three original members (Kenya, Tanzania, and Uganda) in 1999.[84] On July 1, 2010, the community established an EAC Common Market providing for free movement of goods, labor, services and capital within the region.[85] In the agreement, the partner states agreed to eliminate tariff, non-tariff, and technical barriers to trade; harmonize and mutually recognize standards; implement a common trade policy; and ease cross-border movement of persons through an integrated border management system.[86]

West African Economic and Monetary Union (WAEMU)

WAEMU[87] is made up of Benin, Burkina Faso, Côte d'Ivoire, Mali, Niger, Senegal, Togo, and Guinea-Bissau, the sole non-francophone member. This grouping was originally created to promote economic integration among countries that share the CFA franc (*Communauté financière africaine*), a currency formerly tied to the French franc prior to its disappearance in 2000 (but still backed by the French treasury). The member states have espoused the long-term goal of a full economic union with a common market, macroeconomic convergence, regulatory harmonization, and a common investment policy. A preferential tariff arrangement was concluded for member states in 1995, and a customs union with a common external tariff of 22% became operational in 2000. WAEMU countries have established a common accounting system, periodic reviews of member countries' macroeconomic policies, a regional stock exchange, and the legal and regulatory framework for a regional banking system.[88]

APPENDIX B. U.S.–SSA TRADE RELATIONSHIP

Table B-1. SSA Countries Trade Relationship with United States and Preference Program Status

Countries	GSP	GSP-Least Developed	AGOA	AGOA-Lesser Developed	BIT	TIFA
Angola	√	√	√			2009
Benin	√	√	√	√		2002[b]
Botswana	√		√	√		2008[c]
Burkina Faso	√	√	√	√		2002[b]
Burundi	√	√	√			2001[a], 2008[d]
Cameroon	√		√	√	1989	
Cape Verde	√		√	√		
Central African						
Republic	√	√				
Chad	√	√	√	√		
Comoros	√	√	√			2001[a]
Democratic Republic of Congo (Kinshasa)	√	√			1989	2001[a]
Republic of Congo (Brazzaville)	√		√		1994	
Cote d'Ivoire	√		√			2002[b]
Djibouti	√	√	√			2001[a]
Equatorial Guinea						
Eritrea	√					2001[a]
Ethiopia	√	√	√	√		2001[a]
Gabon	√		√			
Gambia	√	√	√	√		
Ghana	√		√	√		1999
Guinea	√	√	√	√		
Guinea-Bissau	√	√	√			2002[b]
Kenya	√		√	√		2001[a], 2008[d]
Lesotho	√	√	√	√		2008c

Table B-1. (Continued)

Countries	GSP	GSP-Least Developed	AGOA	AGOA-Lesser Developed	BIT	TIFA
Liberia	√	√	√	√		2007
Madagascar	√	√				2001[a]
Malawi	√	√	√	√		2001[a]
Mali	√	√	√	√		2002[b]
Mauritania	√	√	√			
Mauritius	√		√	√		2001[a], 2006
Mozambique	√	√	√	√	2005	2005
Namibia	√		√	√		2008[c]
Niger	√	√	√	√		2002b
Nigeria	√		√	√		2000
Rwanda	√	√	√	√	2012	2001[a], 2006, 2008[d]
Sao Tomei and Principe						
Senegal	√		√	√	1990	2002[b]
Seychelles	√		√			2001[a]
Sierra Leone	√	√	√	√		
Somalia	√	√				
South Africa	√		√			1999, 2008[c],2012
South Sudan	√	√				
Sudan						2001[a]
Swaziland	√		√	√		2001[a], 2008[c]
Tanzania	√	√	√	√		2008B
Togo	√	√	√			2002[b]
Uganda	√	√	√	√		2001[a], 2008[d]
Zambia	√	√	√	√		2001[a]
Zimbabwe	√					2001[a]

Source: Analysis by CRS. Data from USTR and USITC.

a. As part of the U.S. TIFA with the Common Market for Eastern and Southern Africa (COMESA).

b. As part of the U.S. TIFA with the West African Economic and Monetary Union (WAEMU).

c. As part of the U.S. Trade, Investment, and Development Cooperation Agreement with the Southern African Customs Union SACU, which is actually a TIDCA

d. As part of the U.S. TIFA with the East African Community (EAC).

End Notes

[1] The White House, *U.S. Strategy Toward Sub-Saharan Africa*, June 2012, p. 4, http://www. whitehouse.gov/sites/ default/files/docs/africa_strategy_2.pdf.

[2] Section 3108 of the Trade Act of 2002, P.L. 107-210.

[3] Section 6002 of the Tax Relief and Health Care Act of 2006, P.L. 109-432.

[4] P.L. 112-163

[5] Jorge Saba Arbache and John Page, "Patterns of Long Term Growth in Sub-Saharan Africa," World Bank, November 2007. Purchasing Power Parity (PPP) estimates attempt to determine comparative prices across countries for similar baskets of goods, taking into account exchange rates and various cost of living measures. This generates an artificial, but uniform, global exchange rate, which can be used to measure the local purchasing value of national currencies.

[6] Jorge Saba Arbache and John Page, "More Growth or Fewer Collapses? A New Look at Long Run Growth in SSA," World Bank, October 2007.

[7] *The Economist*, May 13-19, 2000.

[8] International Monetary Fund *Regional Economic Outlook: Sub-Saharan Africa*, October 2012, http://www.imf.org.

[9] Ibid, p. 95

[10] The World Bank, *Global Development Finance*, 2006 and 2007.

[11] Bureau of Economic Analysis (BEA), Foreign Direct Investment database.

[12] United Nations Conference on Trade and Development, *World Investment Report 2012: Towards a New Generation of Investment Policies*, p. 169.

[13] Based on remarks of representatives from the Chamber of Commerce and GE Africa speaking on U.S. economic engagement in Africa, June 19, 2012.

[14] CRS analysis using the Global Trade Atlas Navigator database.

[15] UNAIDS, *Report on the Global AIDS Epidemic, 2010*, CRS Report R41645, *U.S. Response to the Global Threat of HIV/AIDS: Basic Facts*.

[16] Ibid.

[17] CRS Report RL33584, *AIDS in Africa*, by Nicolas Cook.

[18] See CRS Report R41644, *U.S. Response to the Global Threat of Malaria: Basic Facts*; CRS Report R41802, *The Global Challenge of HIV/AIDS, Tuberculosis, and Malaria*; and CRS Report R41851, *U.S. Global Health Assistance: Background and Issues for the 112th Congress*, by Tiaji Salaam-Blyther.

[19] World Bank Global Development Finance data, http://data.worldbank.org. Foreign debt is defined as total external debt stock, comprising public and publicly guaranteed long-term debt.

[20] International Monetary Fund, *Regional Economic Outlook: Sub-Saharan Africa*, October 2012, http://www.imf.org

[21] United States Trade Representative, 2008 *Comprehensive Report on U.S. Trade and Investment Policy Toward Sub- Saharan Africa and Implementation of the African Growth and Opportunity Act*, May 2008. See also CRS Report RS22534, *The Multilateral Debt Relief Initiative*, by Martin A. Weiss.

[22] CRS Report R40778, *The Global Economic Crisis: Impact on Sub-Saharan Africa and Global Policy Responses*, by Alexis Arieff, Martin A. Weiss, and Vivian C. Jones.

[23] International Monetary Fund, *Regional Economic Outlook*, October 2012, http://www.imf.org.

[24] Contribution from Nicolas Cook, CRS African Affairs Specialist.

[25] Sino-African trade in 2011 also eclipsed the record $104.7 billion in U.S.-African trade attained in 2008.

[26] U.S.-African trade also stood at $29.4 billion in the year 2000 and $94.3 billion in 2011, having increased 221%. In the year 2000, trade with Africa made up 1.5% of total U.S

global trade, and Africa's share had grown to 2.6% by 2011. U.S.-Africa trade peaked in 2008 at $104.7 billion.

[27] Harmonized Tariff Schedule Chapter 27, Mineral Fuels, Mineral Oils and Products of their Distillation; Bituminous Substances; Mineral Waxes. The top five oil suppliers to the United States in 2011 were Canada ($101.9 billion), Saudi Arabia ($46.2 billion), Mexico ($44 billion), Venezuela ($42 billion), and Nigeria ($34 billion) according to U.S. trade statistics (U.S. imports for consumption using the Global Trade Atlas).

[28] CRS calculations based on trade statistics (U.S. imports for consumption) from the U.S. International Trade Commission Trade Dataweb (http://dataweb.usitc.gov) and the Global Trade Atlas trade database.

[29] Harmonized Tariff Schedule Chapter 71, Natural or Cultured Pearls, Precious or Semi-Precious Stones, Precious Metals; Precious Metal Clad Metals, Articles Thereof; Imitation Jewelry; Coin.

[30] CRS calculations based on trade statistics from the U.S. International Trade Commission Trade Dataweb (http://dataweb.usitc.gov).

[31] U.S. International Trade Commission, *Sub-Saharan African Textile and Apparel Inputs: Potential for Competitive Production,* Investigation No. 332-502, May 2009.

[32] Data from the Bureau of Economic Analysis (BEA). Analysis by CRS. BEA industry-specific data were not provided in sufficient detail to break out SSA countries from Africa as a whole.

[33] Ibid.

[34] Ibid.

[35] 76 *Federal Register* 67035.

[36] P.L. 106-200, as amended by §7 of P.L. 108-274.

[37] See CRS Report RL33663, *Generalized System of Preferences: Background and Renewal Debate*, by Vivian C. Jones.

[38] P.L. 93-618, §506A, as added by §111(a) of P.L. 106-200, and as amended by §7 of P.L. 108-274. The USITC conducts a study to determine the import activity and sensitivity of the targeted product(s) from AGOA countries, and reports its determinations to the President. The President may also grant this status, with respect to certain import sensitive articles, to all GSP-qualifying countries.

[39] Department of Commerce, Office of Textiles and Apparel (OTEXA) Summary of AGOA textile and apparel provisions at OTEXA website, http://otexa.ita.doc.gov.

[40] Ibid.

[41] §506A of P.L. 93-618, as added by §111 of P.L. 106-200, and amended by §7 of P.L. 108-274.

[42] Ibid.

[43] For more information, see CRS Report R41922, *Trade Adjustment Assistance (TAA) and Its Role in U.S. Trade Policy*, by J. F. Hornbeck and Laine Elise Rover.

[44] 19 U.S.C. § 3721(c)(3). The statute refers to the International Bank for Reconstruction and Development, one of the five institutions that make up the World Bank Group.

[45] CITA is an interagency group chaired by the Department of Commerce that is responsible for matters affecting textile trade policy and supervising the implementation of all textile trade agreements. CITA was established by Executive Order 11651 on March 3, 1972 (44 *Federal Register* 4699).

[46] The cap for AGOA apparel imports under the special rule for lesser-developed countries is 3.5% of all U.S. apparel articles imported in the previous 12-month period. The cap for all AGOA apparel imports, including those under the special rule, is 7% of all U.S. apparel articles imported in the previous 12-month period.

[47] 77 *Federal Register* 59914, October 1, 2012.

[48] Data from the Office for Textiles and Apparel, Department of Commerce website, http://otexa.ita.doc.gov.

[49] United States Trade Representative website , http://www.ustr.gov/tradeprograms/african-growth-and-opportunity-act-agoa.

[50] CRS calculations based on data from the U.S. International Trade Commission Trade Dataweb, http://dataweb.usitc.gov.

[51] U.S. Census data from the Global Trade Atlas.

[52] U.S. Agency for International Development, Trade Capacity Building Database, http://tcb.eads.usaidallnet.gov/.

[53] Ibid.

[54] Representatives from appropriate Sub-Saharan African regional organizations and government officials from other appropriate countries in Sub-Saharan Africa also could be invited.

[55] Sponsors included the Departments of State, Transportation, and Energy, USDA, USAID, Millennium Challenge Corporation, Export-Import Bank, U.S. Trade and Development Agency, Executive Office of the President, Greater Cincinnati World Affairs Council, Department of Commerce, The Corporate Council on Africa, U.S. Small Business Administration, and U.S. Environmental Protection Agency.

[56] It also provided "structured networking opportunities for African government officials and business leaders with U.S. state and local government officials and business leaders; informational sessions on U.S. government opportunities and services from various federal agencies; and site visits to companies and organizations." State Department, *U.S.-Africa Business Conference 2012*.

[57] CRS Report 98-567, *The Overseas Private Investment Corporation: Background and Legislative Issues*, by Shayerah Ilias.

[58] CRS Report R42472, *Export-Import Bank: Background and Legislative Issues*, by Shayerah Ilias.

[59] Export-Import Bank Reauthorization Act, 12 U.S.C. 635(b)(9)(B)(iii).

[60] Export-Import Bank of the United States, *2011 Annual Report*, http://www.exim.gov/about/reports/ar/2011/exim_2011annualreport.pdf.

[61] Ibid.

[62] *Powering Export Growth*, U.S. Commercial Service Annual Report, 2011.

[63] The Commerce and State departments agreed to expand this program additional 11 countries in September 2011.

[64] AGOA, §125(a)(4).

[65] AGOA, §125(b).

[66] U.S. Commercial Service, *Powering Export Growth*, U.S. Commercial Service Annual Report, 2011.CS staff are also located in Cairo, Egypt; Tripoli, Libya; and Casablanca, Morocco.

[67] U.S. Trade and Development Agency, *2010 Annual Report*. Examples of specific USTDA projects in SSA are available on the USTDA website at http://www.ustda.gov/program/regions/subsaharanafrica/.

[68] Enhanced Integrated Framework website, http://www.enhancedif.org/documents/ EIF%20toolbox/ EIF%20Trust%20Fund%20Current%20Status.pdf.

[69] 2008 USTR Report, p. 40.

[70] Ibid.

[71] SACU countries are Botswana, Lesotho, Namibia, South Africa, and Swaziland.

[72] U.S. International Trade Representative website, http://www.ustr.gov.

[73] Ibid.

[74] International Monetary Fund, *International Financial Statistics*, retrieved from Economist Intelligence Unit *All Country Data database*.

[75] U.S. International Trade Commission data website, at http://dataweb.usitc.gov.

[76] 2008 USTR SSA Report, p. 42.

[77] COMESA is made up of Burundi, Comoros, Democratic Republic of Congo, Djibouti, Egypt, Eritrea, Ethiopia, Kenya, Libya, Madagascar, Malawi, Mauritius, Rwanda, Seychelles, South Sudan, Sudan, Swaziland, Uganda, Zambia, and Zimbabwe.

[78] WAEMU/UEMOA members are Benin, Burkina Faso, Cape Verde, Cote d'Ivoire, Gambia, Ghana, Guinea-Bissau, Liberia, Mali, Niger, Nigeria, Senegal, Sierra Leone, and Togo.

[79] Ibid.

[80] U.S. Trade Representative website, http://www.ustr.gov/trade

[81] European Union, *EU's First Economic Partnership with an African Region Goes Live*, Press Release, May 14, 2012, http://europa.eu/newsroom/press-releases/index_en.htm.

[82] In 2003, the President declared Eritrea and the Central African Republic to be ineligible for AGOA. In 2004, Cote d'Ivoire was declared ineligible as well, but was reinstated in 2011. In 2009, benefits for Guinea, Madagascar, and Niger were terminated because the President determined that they were not making continual progress in meeting AGOA requirements (Guinea and Niger were reinstated in 2011). Also in 2009, Mauritania was removed from AGOA eligibility, but was reinstated later that year. Lesotho, which is considered an AGOA success story, has been the subject of persistent complaints from indigenous labor groups regarding working conditions in newly developed textile plants. In some years, Swaziland has received warnings from the State Department that its human rights record does not meet AGOA eligibility requirements. Several countries have questionable commitment to privatization and tariff reform.

[83] Common Market for Eastern and Southern Africa (COMESA) website.

[84] East African Community (EAC) website, http://www.eac.int.

[85] Ibid.

[86] Ibid.

[87] WAEMU is also known as UEMOA from its French name, *Union Economique et Monetaire Oest-Africaine*.

[88] 2008 USTR SSA Report, p. 39.

In: The African Growth and Opportunity Act ISBN: 978-1-62948-299-6
Editors: H. Sarisohn and J. Cohen

Chapter 3

STATEMENT OF AMBASSADOR JOHNNIE CARSON, ASSISTANT SECRETARY FOR AFRICAN AFFAIRS, U.S. DEPARTMENT OF STATE. HEARING ON "ECONOMIC STATECRAFT: EMBRACING AFRICA'S MARKET POTENTIAL"*

Mr. Chairman and Members of the Committee:

Thank you for providing me with the opportunity to address the committee on what I feel is an important and timely topic. The U.S. government is committed to expanding trade and investment in sub-Saharan Africa and the numbers show our commitment. U.S. trade to and from Africa has grown significantly in the past ten years. U.S. exports to sub-Saharan Africa tripled from just under $7 billion U.S. dollars in 2001 to over $21 billion dollars in 2011.

As Secretary of State Clinton said at the annual AGOA Forum two weeks ago: "twelve years ago, the United States passed the Africa Growth and Opportunity act because we believed that the countries of Africa had tremendous untapped economic potential that could and should be developed. We shared a vision with many of you of a future in which economic growth in Africa would fuel growth and prosperity worldwide. .trade and investment

* This is an edited, reformatted and augmented version of a Statement presented June 28, 2012 before the Senate Foreign Relations Committee, Subcommittee on African Affairs.

would multiply. .and people across the continent would have new opportunities to start their own businesses, earn higher salaries, improve their lives, and lift the fortunes of their families and communities."

In large part, this vision is becoming reality. It is my firm belief that Africa represents the next global economic frontier. Sub-Saharan Africa continues to weather the global economic crisis more successfully than other regions, and is home to six – and soon to be seven – of the ten fastest growing economies in the world. A recent McKinsey study documented that Africa offers the highest rate of return on foreign investment of any developing region and has for some years now. Consumer spending continues to rise, and 43 percent of Africans currently have discretionary income or could be considered middle class consumers. And a growing middle class is a market for American products – from ipads to Pampers to Caterpillar tractors which increase crop yields to GE turbines which create additional hours of on-grid electricity to Boeing airliners which facilitate African countries' growing links with each other and with other continents.

However, we can do more. Africa's recent economic growth is impressive but the region still only accounts for approximately two percent of global trade. The second pillar of President Obama's recently announced U.S. Strategy Toward Sub-Saharan Africa directs the Administration to "spur economic growth, trade and investment in sub-Saharan Africa." This new approach recognizes that it is in the interest of both the United States and our African partners to improve the region's trade competitiveness, encourage the diversification of exports beyond natural resources, and ensure sustained economic growth which benefits all sectors of society.

This new strategy elevates economic growth, trade and investment issues by calling for increased U.S. focus to (1) promote an enabling environment for trade and investment ; (2) improve economic governance; (3) promote regional integration; (4) expand African capacity to effectively access and benefit from global markets; and (5) encourage U.S. companies to trade with and invest in Africa.

In addition to the President's new U.S. Strategy Toward Sub-Saharan Africa, our efforts to increase our commercial engagement in Africa are firmly in line with Secretary Clinton's global focus on Economic Statecraft. The State Department's economic statecraft policy harnesses the forces of global economics to advance our diplomatic agenda and puts the tools of our diplomacy to work to meet our economic goals. We are committed to using every opportunity available to advance not only diplomatic and political priorities but our economic and commercial goals as well. I would like to highlight a few of the programs that the Bureau of African Affairs has been working on as we shift our economic orientation towards Africa from focusing almost exclusively on development assistance to promoting sustained economic growth through private sector, commercial, trade and investment activities.

The African Growth and Opportunity Act continues to be the centerpiece of our trade policy with sub-Saharan Africa. It is Africa's most important vehicle for market access and its unilateral trade preferences have created enormous goodwill for the United States on the continent. As you know, many African countries are not taking full advantage of the benefits of AGOA. However, some AGOA beneficiary countries take good advantage of the provisions for fabric and apparel product lines. The third country fabric provision component of AGOA was designed to provide an opportunity for AGOA-qualified countries to be more competitive in labor intensive textile processes such as sewing, stitching and cutting fabric.

It was widely recognized that most African countries were not able to compete in the more capital intensive process of producing fabric from raw cotton.

African manufacturers have successfully used the AGOA third country fabric provision to create jobs, not just in the manufacturing countries but have used this provision to create cross-border pan-African supply chains. These supply chains also encourage regional integration – one of our key goals for the continent. Fabric and apparel exports are the second largest AGOA export after extractive industry products. However, these imports still account for less than two percent of U.S. imports.

I'd like to say a few words about what is likely to happen if third country fabric legislation is not renewed. In our globally linked world, American buyers place orders six to nine to twelve months ahead. 95 percent of AGOA apparel and textile exports enter under the third country provision. And the AGOA third country fabric provision is the only way that African textile and apparel companies can remain competitive with larger producers such as China, Vietnam and Bangladesh.

Without our help, jobs will continue to disappear in some of Africa's most vulnerable economies, affecting primarily women and the families they support. 85 percent of these imports come from just four countries: Lesotho, Kenya, Mauritius and Swaziland. I know that diplomats from these countries have come to see you to emphasize the disproportionate effect that lack of renewal of this provision will have on their economies.

The effects of the loss of orders are troubling. At the AGOA Forum, the Swazi Minister for Trade told AGOA delegates that the loss of the provision will "shut the country down". The textile and apparel sector is the largest formal sector employer with over 15, 000 jobs and employment is already 41 percent in this small, landlocked country. Loss of just one of these jobs means that ten people lose their livelihood, since Swazi officials calculate that each textile job directly supports ten people. Lack of orders have already led to plants closures in Namibia, robbing people of their legitimate livelihoods and governments of much needed tax revenues. The Mauritians report that their orders are down 30 percent since January due to the uncertainty whether this provision will be renewed in a timely fashion.

Madagascar's loss of AGOA eligibility in 2009 is a possible model of what could happen if this provision were to expire. Prior to its loss of AGOA eligibility, Madagascar was one of the top textile producing countries in Africa, exporting over $2050 million in textiles in 2007. Due to 2009 coup, the government of Madagascar lost all AGOA benefits, including the textile provision. Apparel exports plummeted by $150 million in 2010. This more than $150 million drop in textile exports resulted in the loss of 50,000 jobs which will more than likely never return.

We continue to actively educate, inform and encourage U.S. companies to be more active in Africa. This is a continent on the move and there are enormous opportunities for U.S. companies to enter the market, make money, and create jobs for Americans here at home.

In February, I led a trade mission to Mozambique, Tanzania, Nigeria and Ghana with 10 U.S. energy companies ready to do business. A lack of reasonably priced reliable power remains one of the most binding constraints to economic growth throughout Africa. Governments across the continent are working to attract new trade and foreign investment that will sustain their rapid economic growth and build their middle class. The goal of this mission was to highlight opportunities for U.S. companies and help address a glaring need for increased power sector infrastructure in Africa. The mission was a success and a number of these U.S. companies concluded partnership agreements with African companies to jointly develop power projects. Ex-Im Bank and USTDA representatives also participated in the mission to ensure that both the U.S. participants and our Africa partners are fully aware of U.S. financing options. We are in the process of putting together a trade mission to accompany the Secretary to South Africa for the U.S.- South Africa Strategic Dialogue. In addition, I plan to lead similar trade missions in the future and continue to help and encourage U.S. companies to be a part of the growing economic dynamism of Africa.

In our continuing efforts to inform, educate and encourage U.S. companies to pursue commercial opportunities on the continent, just last week, the State Department, in collaboration with the Department of Commerce's U.S. Export Assistance Center in Cincinnati, the Department of Transportion, the Ex-Im Bank, USTDA, USAID USTR, and several other U.S. Government agencies, hosted a U.S.-Africa Business Conference in Cincinnati, Ohio. This conference attracted well over 400 participants, including African government officials, and representatives from the U.S. and African private sectors and civil society. The U.S.-Africa Business Conference expanded on the AGOA Forum infrastructure theme by focusing on infrastructure development, including energy, transportation, and water and sanitation. It showcased U.S. business expertise to potential African clients and highlighted trade and investment opportunities in Africa to U.S. exporters and investors through structured networking opportunities for African government officials and business leaders with U.S. state and local government officials and business leaders; informational sessions on U.S. government opportunities and services from various federal agencies; and site visits to companies and research facilities highlighting potential technologies for Africa.

Cincinnati was selected as the conference location for its potential to increase commercial partnerships with Africa at local, state, and regional levels given its concentration of Fortune 500 and 1000 companies. I am pleased that the Cincinnati conference built on the successes of the 2010 Kansas City, Missouri business conference. Bringing African government officials and private sector representatives outside of the beltway allows us to more effectively focus on business to business linkages.

We also have two very popular programs which develop business capacity in Africa, the African Women's Entrepreneurship Program (AWEP) and the President's Young African Leaders Initiative. This year delegates from both programs participated in both our AGOA Forum and US-Africa Business Conference events. AWEP is an outreach, education and engagement initiative that targets African women entrepreneurs to promote business growth, increase trade both regionally and to the United States using AGOA, create better business environments, and empower African women entrepreneurs to become voices of change in their communities. The State Department organizes an annual AWEP professional exchange program for these women to improve their skills and has created a series of public-private partnerships with ExxonMobil, Intel, Vital Voices and the Cherie Blair Foundation for Women.

This year's President's Young African Leaders Initiative included the Innovation Youth Summit and Mentoring Partnership with Young African Leaders and brought more than 60 participants to the U.S. for three weeks of professional exchange and entrepreneurial hands-on training. This initiative encourages U.S.- Africa collaboration to promote business innovation, investment and corporate social responsibility activities in Africa.

However, there are still many barriers that stand in the way of companies that hope to do business there. In many places, corruption is too common. The cost of finance, including investment finance, is too high. Infrastructure is lacking or inadequate. Regulatory systems are often inconsistent and inefficient. Also, many U.S. businesses see African markets as too risky. The perception of Africa as poverty filled and strife ridden persists. We work closely with African governments so that they will continue to enact the kinds of reforms to support improved investment climates which will attract both domestic and foreign investment. In addition, we continue to highlight opportunities for trade and investment in the region for U.S. companies and to work with them to conclude deals. Our work with GE Transportation in Ghana on a locomotive tender where GE was ultimately able to win a deal worth $200 million in U.S. content is but one example. We are confident that the U.S. can compete effectively in Africa, but we have to continue to encourage American companies to go to Africa and we have to encourage African countries to continue to make their regulatory and business environment more conducive for American business. Greater U.S.-Africa trade is in the interest of both America and Africa.

Mr. Chairman and Members of the Committee, I want to thank you for the opportunity to appear before you today. I will be happy to answer any questions you have.

In: The African Growth and Opportunity Act ISBN: 978-1-62948-299-6
Editors: H. Sarisohn and J. Cohen

Chapter 4

STATEMENT OF EARL W. GAST, ASSISTANT ADMINISTRATOR FOR AFRICA, U.S. AGENCY FOR INTERNATIONAL DEVELOPMENT. HEARING ON "ECONOMIC STATECRAFT: EMBRACING AFRICA'S MARKET POTENTIAL"*

Good morning Chairman Coons, Ranking Member Isakson, and members of the Subcommittee. It is my pleasure to appear before you again.

Sub-Saharan Africa is one of the fastest growing regions in the world. In 2011, it was home to six of the world's 10 fastest growing economies. Foreign direct investment is approaching $80 billion a year, and trade has tripled over the last decade. Consumer spending is set to rise 80 percent by 2020 and Africa now has a fast-growing middle class, expected to increase from 60 million to 100 million people by 2015.

The continent's fortune is not the outcome of good luck. It is the result of years of hard work and better macroeconomic management; improved economic and political governance; a reduction in armed conflicts; increasing foreign capital inflows, particularly direct investment; and improvements in the business climate.

The President's strategy toward Sub-Saharan Africa, released June 14 to coincide with the African Growth and Opportunity Act (AGOA) Forum,

* This is an edited, reformatted and augmented version of a statement presented June 28, 2012 before the Senate Foreign Relations Committee, Subcommittee on African Affairs.

renews our emphasis on spurring economic growth, trade, and investment in Africa, including promoting an enabling environment for trade and investment, regional integration, improved economic governance and expanded African capacity to trade. As America supports the development of Africa's economic growth, it can generate new export markets and tap into a common market that could one day outpace India or China.

Yet the commodity boom in resource-rich countries has not yet succeeded in generating strong, positive, economy-wide spill-over effects to other sectors or neighboring countries. And resource-poor states remain on the sidelines, constrained by their inability to mobilize domestic resources as well as attract external resources—apart from official aid flows that sustain a minimum level of investment that prevents the development process from stalling altogether. Their small, expensive markets keep them isolated from the dynamic changes occurring from globalized markets. Domestic firms often miss out on technical expertise, technology transfer and productivity gains from foreign direct investment. Market informality and a limited tax base limit many countries' domestic resource base.

Nor has Africa's growth translated into meaningful development and poverty reduction. Basic infrastructure lags far behind that of other developing regions; the African Development Bank estimates that inadequate infrastructure suppresses Africa's per capita growth rate by as much as two percentage points a year. Political fragility, ethnic conflict, and food insecurity plague even the most stable economies such as Kenya and South Africa.

Trade openness has been instrumental in the remarkable economic growth in East and Southeast Asia. But Africa has not seen these same benefits; the continent's share in world trade has declined from around 6 percent 25 years ago to approximately 2 percent today. Intra-African trade is not faring much better. More than 80% of Africa's exports are destined for markets outside of Africa; as a contrast, 40 percent of North American trade occurs with other North American countries and 63 percent of Western European trade is among other Western European nations.

A recent World Bank report concluded that the continent is losing billions of dollars in potential trade earnings every year because of high trade barriers with neighboring countries. Procedures and regulations vary by country, which, coupled with a lack of infrastructure, significantly increases the time and cost required to ship goods across borders. In some cases, it is less expensive to ship a container of goods to Nairobi from Europe than from Lagos. The implications are far-reaching: huge opportunities are lost for specialization and value addition. Production and export structures oriented to primary commodities—minerals, timber, coffee, cocoa, oil, gas—often come at the cost of high-value products that would provide broad-based benefits and create jobs.

Many African governments recognize the detrimental impact of high trade barriers. Throughout the continent, they are working to build bridges across geographical boundaries to create important economic trade regions. Although regional agreements vary, and often overlap, all have the goal of reducing complicated trade barriers among member countries. African regional economic communities have launched various trade liberalization initiatives to stabilize and remove barriers to trade, harmonize customs duties and internal taxes, facilitate trade through information and promotional services and abolish restrictions to the movement of people, goods, services, and investments across borders.

AGOA is the cornerstone of the U.S.-Africa commercial relationship, and is the most generous bilateral trade legislation the United States has ever enacted. AGOA is a key tool in U.S. efforts to foster development of the next generation of emerging markets, which includes building effective trading partnerships between the United States and the countries of sub-Saharan Africa. It provides substantial trade preferences that, along with those under the Generalized System of Preferences and Most-Favored Nation tariff treatment, allow almost all goods produced in the AGOA-eligible countries to enter the U.S. market duty-free. AGOA offers tangible incentives for African countries to continue their efforts to open their economies and build free markets. Promoting prosperity, open markets, and good governance in Africa through programs like AGOA, has improved the trade environment for both U.S. and African businesses and spurred economic growth.

It has worked. Since 2001, exports under AGOA have increased more than 500 percent, from $8.15 billion in 2001 to $53.8 billion in 2011. About 90 percent of these exports have been oil, which underscores Africa's growing strategic importance to the United States. At the same time, under AGOA, the volume of non-energy exports to the United States—that critical engine for growth in jobs and economic development in Africa—has increased 275 percent, from $1.2 billion to $4.5 billion between 2001 and 2011. Paul Ryberg, the president of the African Coalition on Trade, which has companies and trade organizations in 19 African countries, estimates that as many as 1.3 million jobs have been created indirectly by AGOA, supporting up to 10 million people. Many of these jobs are held by women—a vital building block for development given that African women are more likely to invest job-related income in the food security, health, and education of their families.

In May 2011, the U.N. Economic Commission for Africa conducted a survey in Africa of AGOA's benefits. Three-quarters of the responding companies viewed AGOA as "very important" (58 percent) or "important" (17 percent). Seventy-five percent of the companies indicated that AGOA had contributed to job creation and capacity building, and a majority of the respondents emphasized the importance of business support services, such as greater technical assistance for conforming with Sanitary and Phytosanitary Standards, and promoting African products in the U.S. market.

Trade capacity building has been central to USAID's work to achieve our development objectives on the continent, particularly the realization of the Millennium Development Goals (MDGs). MDG 1, to eradicate extreme hunger and poverty, is furthered by achieving full, productive, decent employment for all, especially women and young people. Trade and trade agreements increase productive, value added employment opportunities beyond what a self-contained, subsistence economy can provide. It also reduces the proportion of people who suffer from hunger, because free trade, in the context of sound agricultural policy and global integration, balances the differences in natural endowments and labor productivity. Trade also contributes to MDG 8, to develop a global partnership for development, by nurturing an open, rule-based, predictable, non-discriminatory trading and financial system.

Additionally, there is an unavoidable link between the international trading regime and the enjoyment of human rights. The UN Office of the High Commissioner for Human Rights has found that economic growth through free trade increases the resources available for the realization of human rights. Countries do not qualify for AGOA unless they are determined to have established, or made continual progress toward establishing the rule of law and political pluralism; combating corruption; enacting policies to reduce poverty and increase the availability of health care and educational opportunities; protecting human rights and worker rights; and eliminating certain child labor practices.

An extensive study—"From Aid to Trade: Delivering Results"—conducted in November 2010 found a statistically significant relationship between USAID trade capacity-building obligations and developing country export. Specifically it found that an additional $1 of USAID trade competitiveness assistance is associated with a $42 increase in the value of developing county exports within two years. In addition, USAID support for trade and investment in Africa provides a significant contribution to trade negotiations conducted by the U.S. Trade Representative.

Over the past 10 years, USAID programs have improved the enabling environment for U.S. trade with sub-Saharan Africa; empowered African small and medium-sized enterprises to increase their exports to U.S., regional, and international markets; and facilitated regional economic integration. Between 2006 and 2010, USAID's African Global Competitiveness Initiative supported over $5 billion in non-petroleum exports; leveraged $2.8 billion for energy, information and communication technologies, and transportation infrastructure, resulting in over 1.35 million Africans gaining access to the internet.

At the regional level, USAID efforts for an improved enabling environment have helped to advance cross-border integration and boost intra- and extra-regional trade—work primarily carried out by USAID's three Trade Hubs located in Botswana, Ghana, and Kenya. These Hubs have implemented innovative and important initiatives to reduce both legal and illicit bottlenecks along major trade corridors, establish single border posts, and computerized customs procedures.

An analysis by the Organization for Economic Cooperation and Development and the World Trade Organization in 2011 concluded that USAID's Trade Hubs had been largely successful in developing best practices in customs procedures, processes and technology. They have helped speed up customs clearances in Mozambique, improved customs procedures in Southern Africa, and established a model for regional economic commissions to harmonize standards, monitor compliance with trade protocols, and facilitate the analysis of technical trade issues. Combined, these initiatives have reduced the time, cost, and red tape long associated with trading in Africa.

USAID's Trade Hubs count many successes. The Southern Africa Trade Hub's efforts to extend border operating hours along the Trans Kalahari Corridor, introduce a single customs declaration, and implement a corridor performance management system, contributed to an increase in a twelvefold usage of the corridor and a reduction in travel time from 72 to 48 hours. In East Africa, USAID support for customs reform in 2010 resulted in the implementation of a common customs software platform that allows customs officials to communicate virtually across borders. This reduced the time it takes to transport goods along the Mombasa-Kigali trade corridor by five days and reduced the cost of trading goods in the East Africa region by 2 percent, despite a 19.2 percent increase in fuel cost in 2010.

At the Sleek Garments factory in Accra, Ghana, a sign overlooks a bustling assembly line of 300 workers: "Quality First, Quantity Second." Sleek's founder and CEO, Nora Bannerman, has held to that philosophy since she began her career as a fashion designer 30 years ago. And she is determined to maintain it as Sleek shifts into mass production, stitching casual shirts and work uniforms for some of the largest retail chains in the United States. Sleek is part of Ghana's blossoming apparel manufacturing cluster, which has been encouraged by the government to relocate and build several clothing factories. Many of these factories export to the United States under AGOA's Third Country Fabric provision, which has provided hundreds of thousands of jobs across Sub-Saharan Africa. USAID's West Africa Trade Hub helped to put Ghana on the radar as an exporter of high-quality garments by connecting Bannerman with international buyers, providing financial planning services, and advising her on pre-export financing to purchase fabric for her orders.

The Presitex garment company in Lesotho was growing and looking for ways to keep expanding its operations and was especially interested in taking advantage of AGOA so it could begin exporting to the United States. At the same time, clothing manufacturers in South Africa were looking for regional suppliers of textiles and other clothing inputs, like yarn. Presitex used to source from Asia, but, needing to reduce transport costs, it turned to USAID's Southern Africa Trade Hub for help. The Hub put Presitex in touch with a knitting mill in South Africa and helped them to negotiate a $1.2 million annual deal. Lesotho's apparel industry has grown to become especially successful under AGOA—at one time supporting 50,000 jobs. And regional integration is considered critical for the survival of Lesotho's apparel industry, both to maintain job opportunities in Lesotho and as a platform for future economic growth.

When 24 private sector stakeholders and the USAID West Africa Trade Hub co-founded the African Cashew Alliance (ACA) five years ago, its mandate was simple and clear: to increase cashew processing in West Africa in order to create jobs and reduce poverty. The opening of six new major processing facilities over the last six months—which will employ as many as 5,000 people—is yet more evidence that the Alliance is a success. The ACA today includes over 135 members from 23 countries, including every African cashew-producing country and buyers and retailers from every major international market. In a recent ACA survey of its members found that more than 80 percent had used the Alliance's services to grow their business.

Bringing together every aspect of the industry has allowed international buyers to quickly assess the opportunities—and act. "None of our business in Africa would have been possible without the ACA," said Shalin Behal of IRACEMA, a leading processor from Brazil that has purchased millions of dollars of African cashews. "The ACA has introduced us to all the key players in the region, facilitated field trips and all our first steps in doing business here." The impacts in the communities where the processing facilities are located are significant. Residents of a town in Côte d'Ivoire said prostitution, once a problem in the community, had all but disappeared once the factory opened. This was attributed to the hundreds of jobs that were created for young women—some of the almost 10,000 cashew processing jobs ACA has created in West Africa.

Under the President's new Strategy toward Sub-Saharan Africa, USAID's work will capitalize on Africa's steadily rising middle class and burgeoning opportunities, particularly in finance and infrastructure, to promote U.S. trade and investment in the region. USAID is uniquely positioned to take a major role in the implementation of the President's strategy, particularly spurring economic growth, trade and investment. Staff in both Washington and the field have a deep knowledge of the African economic scene, both in terms of macroeconomic conditions and in terms of what businesses need to be successful in Africa. USAID has supported macro and micro policy reform, key to accelerating growth; built the capacity for policy analysis in both government and the private sector; and strengthened various institutions of economic governance such as bank supervision, tax collection, and commercial courts.

Many of USAID's programs have focused on analyzing the constraints to private sector development and to helping remove existing obstacles, both directly and through empowering businesses and business associations to bring the obstacles the face to the attention of their governments. USAID also has strong relationships with both the U.S. and African business communities; USAID implements a number of programs that provide information and link U.S. investors to opportunities in Africa, including the Africa Infrastructure Program. It provides specialized advisors to African governments to address legal, financial, regulatory, and other constraints preventing private sector investment in energy infrastructure. In the past three years alone, these efforts have leveraged over $700 million in private sector investment in the energy sector, with an emphasis on clean energy.

USAID's newest trade and investment initiative—the African Competitiveness and Trade Expansion (ACTE) Initiative, announced in 2011—is furthering the progress USAID has made, and supports the President's new U.S. Strategy toward Sub-Saharan Africa. Through USAID's three Trade Hubs, ACTE focuses on the role African governments, businesses, and civil society play in advancing regional and international trade, increasing the international competitiveness of key value chains, and promoting trade and investment between the United States and Africa and within Africa.

USAID established the Private Capital Group for Africa (PCGA) in 2011 to help deploy Agency resources and tools to leverage private investment. For every U.S. assistance dollar, PCGA activities are anticipated to leverage $30 in private capital to support key development goals. For example, in West Africa we are supporting the formation of a lending company to be co-owned by U.S. companies to support supply chains in the region. We are also working to link a U.S. investment company with Kenyan pension funds to co-invest in small and medium-sized enterprises in Africa. With just an $18 million investment from USAID, this partnership has the potential to catalyze over $500 million in private funds that will support the expansion of over 500 enterprises, provide sustainable livelihoods to over 100,000 smallholder farmers, and support 42,000 jobs in sub-Saharan Africa. One of PCGA's early successes was the launch of the Partners Forum, a group of U.S. leaders of industry (in particular those from the investment sector) who provide advice on how to best engage with the private sector and align business and development goals. The Forum represents our commitment to continuous engagement with the private sector to identify where priorities align and partnerships are possible.

At the same time, USAID's Partnership for Growth aligns with these broader U.S. priorities for trade and investment among countries that have a proven, positive track record in policy and development. Our alliances with Ghana and Tanzania are generating investment and trade opportunities for U.S. energy companies, increasing the availability and consistent supply of energy for U.S. companies operating in those countries, supporting regional integration to develop economically attractive markets, and facilitating increased trade opportunities in Ghana.

Looking forward, green technologies offer another promising opportunity to expand U.S.-Africa trade. A 2011 report by Frost & Sullivan—"Mega Trends in Africa: A Bright Vision for the Growing Continent"—suggests that investment in renewable energy in the continent will rise to $57 billion by 2020 as interest in wind, solar and geothermal power soars. Consequently, at this year's AGOA Forum, USAID and the U.S. Geothermal Energy Association publicly announced their partnership to help develop East Africa's geothermal resources. The extensive geothermal sources found along the East Africa Rift Valley not only has the potential to provide clean power for African economies, but also a significant spur for investment and cooperation between U.S. and African energy companies. USAID plans to continue to make innovative public-private partnerships like this one to support development while also opening new markets for the U.S. investment.

Spurring economic growth, trade, and investment, along with promoting opportunity and development, are two pillars of the President's strategy toward sub-Saharan Africa, and they are inextricably linked. Inclusive economic growth, trade and investment are imperative to achieving lasting, durable development. USAID will bring to bear all of its strengths catalyzing growth through public-private partnerships, leveraging private capital and investment, harnessing onthe-ground and industry knowledge, and leveling the playing field for domestic and international entry to implement the new Presidential Policy Directive on Sub-Saharan Africa.

Thank you for inviting me to speak with you today on this critical issue, and I welcome any questions you might have.

In: The African Growth and Opportunity Act ISBN: 978-1-62948-299-6
Editors: H. Sarisohn and J. Cohen

Chapter 5

STATEMENT OF FLORIZELLE LISER, ASSISTANT U.S. TRADE REPRESENTATIVE FOR AFRICA, OFFICE OF THE U.S. TRADE REPRESENTATIVE. HEARING ON "ECONOMIC STATECRAFT: EMBRACING AFRICA'S MARKET POTENTIAL"*

INTRODUCTION

Chairman Coons, Ranking Member Isakson, and other distinguished members of the subcommittee, thank you for the opportunity to speak with you today about the Obama Administration's strategy to encourage economic growth, trade and investment in Africa. We welcome your interest in and support for advancing the U.S. trade and investment relationship with sub-Saharan Africa.

---

* This is an edited, reformatted and augmented version of a statement presented June 28, 2012 before the Senate Foreign Relations Committee, Subcommittee on African Affairs.

The Administration's Strategy for Sub-Saharan Africa

On June 14, 2012, President Obama approved a new Presidential Policy Directive (PPD) for sub-Saharan Africa. To advance U.S. interests in Africa, the strategy sets forth four strategic objectives: (1) strengthen democratic institutions; (2) spur economic growth, trade and investment; (3) advance peace and security; and (4) promote opportunity and development.

The new strategy commits the United States to be proactive in the face of the numerous challenges and opportunities facing sub-Saharan Africa. In particular, it directs the United States to expand our efforts to increase economic growth, trade, and investment. USTR is part of an interagency effort - building on the successes of the partnerships we have built in previous years - to foster sustained economic growth and to promote U.S. trade and investment with sub-Saharan Africa.

Spurring Economic Growth, Trade and Investment

Sub-Saharan Africa is expected to grow by more than 5 percent this year, and between 2000 and 2010, 6 of the 10 fastest-growing countries in the world were in Sub-Saharan Africa. Sustained economic growth has the potential to lift millions out of poverty and foster long-term stability. Today's challenge is to ensure that these gains continue and are spread across the continent. The Administration's new strategy addresses these challenges by calling for increased U.S. focus to spur economic growth through expanded trade and investment by (1) promoting an enabling environment for trade and investment; (2) improving economic governance; (3) promoting regional integration; (4) expanding African capacity to effectively access and benefit from global markets; and (5) encouraging U.S. companies to trade with and invest in Africa.

This approach recognizes that it is in the interest of the United States and our African partners to promote regional integration, create new trade and investment opportunities for African and U.S. firms, encourage the diversification of African exports beyond natural resources, and ensure that the benefits from growth are broad-based.

AGOA AND THE THIRD COUNTRY FABRIC PROVISION

AGOA is the cornerstone of America's trade and investment policy with sub-Saharan Africa. AGOA's performance and effectiveness are closely tied to its Third-Country Fabric (TCF) provision, which is set to expire in September 2012. The TCF provision is crucial to the continued survival of Africa's textile and apparel industry – it has generated hundreds of thousands of jobs in sub-Saharan Africa, including in least developed countries, and has helped American retailers reduce their costs, diversify their supply chains, and provide greater low-cost apparel options for U.S. consumers. Swift passage of legislation extending AGOA's TCF provision is necessary and its extension urgently needed to ensure AGOA's continued success – and the stability, development, and economic growth of sub-Saharan African countries. We applaud Congress' recent agreement to advance AGOA's third country fabric provision, and appreciate the work that members of this Committee have undertaken to move this important provision forward.

Beyond apparel, AGOA is a measurable success. Total two-way trade between the United States and sub-Saharan Africa has increased by over 300 percent since AGOA was enacted in 2000. U.S. imports under AGOA have increased by over 500 percent from 2001 (the first full-year of AGOA trade). Petroleum imports dominate this trade, but non-petroleum AGOA trade has tripled to nearly $5 billion in 2011, spurred by significant growth of nontraditional, value-added products such as apparel, cut flowers, fruits and nuts, wines, cocoa, and footwear. AGOA apparel imports have doubled, and today about twice the number of eligible countries are shipping non-commodity goods under AGOA than they were a decade ago. Additionally, U.S. exports to sub-Saharan Africa have more than tripled since 2001. These exports support thousands of U.S. jobs and help African countries to modernize their economies.

The Obama Administration is committed to working with Congress toward a seamless renewal of AGOA beyond 2015 to provide the predictability needed for U.S. and African businesses, entrepreneurs, buyers, and investors to continue to reap the benefits of AGOA. The Administration is consulting with Africa trade stakeholders, including Congress, African government officials, U.S. and African private sector, and civil society representatives on modifications needed to make AGOA more effective and mutually beneficial.

PROMOTING U.S.-SUB-SAHARAN AFRICA TRADE AND INVESTMENT

As an office within the Executive Office of the President, USTR is responsible for coordinating and leading the interagency engagement with our sub-Saharan partners on trade and investment issues, including under our Trade and Investment Framework Agreements (TIFAs) with individual countries and regional organizations. U.S. TIFAs provide a formal mechanism for a high-level engagement to address bilateral issues and to help enhance U.S.-sub-Saharan Africa trade and investment relations. The United States has eleven TIFA partners in sub-Saharan Africa: Angola, Ghana, Liberia, Mauritius, Mozambique, Nigeria, Rwanda, South Africa, the East African Community (EAC), the Common Market for East and Southern Africa (COMESA), and the West African Economic and Monetary Union (UEMOA). The United States also has a Trade, Investment, and Development Cooperative Agreement with the five countries of the Southern African Customs' Union (SACU).

In addition, the Obama Administration is pursuing a new trade and investment partnership with the EAC, which is one of the most cohesive and ambitious regional economic groupings in sub-Saharan Africa. At a recent meeting which Ambassador Kirk and senior administration officials held with the EAC Secretary General and Trade Ministers, the United States and the EAC agreed to explore under the partnership, a regional investment treaty, a trade facilitation agreement, continued U.S. trade capacity building assistance, and a commercial dialogue. We are working closely with the Commerce Department to move forward on the commercial dialogue, which would create practical ways in which U.S. and EAC governments can work together and with our respective business communities. These agreements and other activities under the partnership will help to promote EAC regional integration and economic growth, and to expand and diversify U.S.-EAC trade and investment. They could also serve as building blocks towards a more comprehensive trade agreement over the long term.

In the toolbox of U.S. Government initiatives to improve the attractiveness of an economy's investment climate, perhaps none is more powerful than an investment treaty. Bilateral investment treaties (BITs) help protect U.S. investment and help promote economic growth by encouraging market-based economic reform and the policies that make doing business in Africa more attractive for U.S. businesses. These agreements establish a framework of reciprocal protections that include nondiscriminatory treatment; free transfer of investment-related funds; prompt, adequate, and effective compensation in the event of an expropriation; and transparency in governance. U.S. BITs also give investors the right to bring investment disputes to neutral, international arbitration panels.

The United States has BITs in force with six countries in sub-Saharan Africa, and the region has become a locus for recent U.S. BIT activity. Our most recently concluded BIT was with Rwanda – an agreement that entered into force on January 1st of this year. We hope that our most recently launched BIT negotiation with Mauritius will soon conclude, and we are actively pursuing BIT discussions with other countries in the region, including with the members of the East African Community in the context of our EAC Partnership, and with Ghana.

The Administration recognizes the importance of African regional integration and intra-African trade. Facilitating intra-African trade, reducing barriers to such trade, and harmonizing investment and trade rules will build economies of scale, improve African competitiveness, and attract investment to the region. Thus, we are supporting African regional integration through a number of initiatives designed to build trade capacity and promote trade and investment within sub-Saharan Africa, strengthening regional economic communities, forging closer ties with the African Union, and supporting African efforts to establish free trade areas such as the Tripartite initiative (covering COMESA, the EAC, and SADC) and the recently announced Continental Free Trade Area (which is scheduled to be enacted by 2017).

The annual United States-Sub-Saharan Africa Trade and Economic Cooperation Forum (also known as "the AGOA Forum") institutionalizes a high-level dialogue between senior officials of the United States and AGOA beneficiary countries, the private sector and civil society on ways to foster stronger economic ties between the United States and sub-Saharan Africa. The eleventh AGOA Forum was held in Washington D.C. on June 14-15, 2012, with the theme, "Enhancing Africa's Infrastructure for Trade", and other AGOA private sector and civil society events were held in Washington, DC and Cincinnati. As always, the Forum was an important opportunity to discuss the challenges in expanding the U.S.-African trade and investment relationship. Thanks to you Chairman Coons and to Senator Isakson for attending the Forum and meeting with the Ministers to discuss AGOA and pending legislation.

This year's focus on infrastructure was timely. According to the World Bank, the annual requirement for infrastructure expenditure and maintenance in sub-Saharan Africa is about $93 billion a year. However, only about $45 billion is being mobilized, leaving a gap of close to $50 billion annually. This significant funding gap cannot be met by current official sources of funding alone. Private investment could help close the funding gap for Africa's infrastructure. Currently, intraAfrican trade stands at less than 10 percent of African gross domestic product and Africa's share of world trade is only 3 percent. The United States is working with the international community, African governments and the private sector to improve Africa's hard infrastructure - including the roads, ports, power pools, and telecom networks, and Africa's soft infrastructure - such as the laws, regulations and business environment that impact trade and investment decisions. This collaboration is critical because improvements in Africa's infrastructure could significantly advance our efforts to support regional integration, create larger markets for U.S. exports and promote economic growth in Africa.

AFRICA AS A MARKET FOR U.S. BUSINESS

With the continent-wide growth mentioned earlier, Africa presents many opportunities for U.S. businesses. It is a market not yet fully tapped and one that is viewed as a "last frontier" for many global actors such as China, Brazil, India, and the European Union. No other region has rates of return on investment as high as Africa, and it is proving to be a growing investment destination, including for U.S. businesses. And with Africa's growing middle class, youth bulge and undercapitalized entrepreneurs – including many women-owned SMEs, we are focused on increasing U.S. exports to and investment in Africa, and fostering joint ventures that can benefit U.S. businesses – including our own SMEs. Our efforts growing out of the new *U.S. Strategy Toward Sub-Saharan Africa* – including a "Doing Business in Africa Campaign" – will build on existing programs and initiatives such as the National Export Initiative.

CONCLUSION

The Administration is working to strengthen the U.S.-sub-Saharan Africa trade and investment relationship through a range of trade and investment-related initiatives. The new U.S. Strategy toward sub-Saharan Africa builds on this strong foundation and ensures that our trade policy will continue to encourage economic growth, enhance trade and investment, support more jobs in the United States and Africa, and help realize the full potential of the U.S.-sub-Saharan Africa economic partnership.

Thank you.

INDEX

A

B

C

D

F

G

H

M

N

O

P

Q

R

S

T

U

V

W

Y

Z